GEORGE MASON

of Gunston Hall

1725-1792

From a portrait by Boudet after Hesselius
now at Gunston Hall

GEORGE MASON

of Gunston Hall

By

HELEN HILL MILLER

Reproduction of the seal of
GEORGE AND ANN MASON

PUBLISHED BY

THE BOARD OF REGENTS OF GUNSTON HALL

LORTON, VIRGINIA

This booklet is a condensation of *GEORGE MASON,
Constitutionalist,* by Helen Hill (Miller), Harvard
University Press, 1938, now out of print, but available
in many public libraries. The serious student of George
Mason may also find further details of his life and
his influence on American history in *The Life of
George Mason,* by Kate Mason Rowland, published
by G. P. Putnam's Sons, 1892, now out of print, and
in *Glimpse of Glory* by Marian Buckley Cox, published by Garrett & Massie, Inc., Richmond, Virginia,
1954. *Glimpse of Glory* is available at Gunston Hall,
Lorton, Virginia or from the publishers.

LIBRARY OF CONGRESS NO. 58-10081

MANUFACTURED IN THE UNITED STATES OF AMERICA

CONTENTS

GEORGE MASON *of Gunston Hall*

1725-1792

INTRODUCTION

I N the broad heritage of freedom, the documents of the American
Revolution have high place. The Declaration of Rights and State
Constitution adopted in Virginia in 1776 and their counterparts
in colony after colony, the Declaration of Independence, the Federal Constitution, the Bill of Rights enumerated in its first ten amendments, together affirm the basic liberties of a free society, and provide
a frame of government through which common defense, domestic
tranquility and general welfare can be sustained.

None of these instruments bears the name of an author. Most of
them were the joint product of a number of minds. Most of the men
who contributed to their preparation lived on from the colonial into
the Federal period, held national public office, became known by their
records in the country's executive or legislative or judicial affairs.

George Mason of Gunston Hall was an exception. None of the Virginians of the Revolutionary and constitution-making periods took a
more active part than he in framing the basic documents—his proposal
for a Virginia Declaration of Rights was adopted almost without
change. But he repeatedly declined other public responsibilities in Virginia, and he died just as the Federal era was opening a place in national history to his younger contemporaries, Washington and Jefferson,
Madison, Marshall and Monroe. Consequently, the great constitutional
documents in whose drafting he participated, rather than a personal
political record, are his anonymous memorial.

At every critical juncture, over a period of twenty-five years, Mason
produced a public paper of importance:

In 1765, after the British Parliament passed the Stamp Act, his
"Scheme for Replevying Goods Under Distress for Rent," prepared
at the request of George Washington and George William Fairfax,
provided a way to avoid the use of stamped paper for legal bonds.

In 1768, after the Townshend duties were imposed, Mason drew up
a series of draft resolutions, advocating, in reprisal, an economic boycott. The Royal Governor, Lord Botetourt, dissolved the Assembly by
which these proposals were to have been considered, but the Burgesses
reassembled at the Raleigh Tavern and adopted the non-importation
resolution.

In 1772, Mason's "Extracts from the Virginia Charters with Some Remarks Upon Them" provided the brief for American claims of title to the lands beyond the Alleghenies, the territory now comprising the states of Tennessee, Kentucky, Ohio, Indiana, Illinois, Michigan, Wisconsin, and part of Minnesota.

After passage of the Boston Port Act, Mason prepared, and on July 18, 1774, at a meeting of Fairfax County citizens under Washington's chairmanship, read the document that came to be known as the Fairfax Resolves. In these, he developed the issue of taxation without representation; set forth again the merits of non-importation and non-exportation; and proposed appointment of a congress of deputies from all of the colonies, to devise a concerted plan for the preservation of their common rights and to petition the King on behalf of their constitutional privileges. This document was taken by the Fairfax County representatives to Williamsburg in August, and by Virginia's representatives in the first Continental Congress to Philadelphia in September.

A plan produced by Mason and adopted by Fairfax County citizens in September 1774 resulted in the enrollment of volunteers in the Fairfax Independent Company; Washington continued to wear its blue-and-buff uniform as commander-in-chief of the Continental Army.

As the chief author of the Declaration of Rights which the Virginia Convention adopted on June 12, 1776, Mason produced a document which became a model for similar declarations in other American colonies, directly influenced the "déclaration des droits de l'homme" of the French Revolutionaries in 1789, and reappeared in the bill of rights appended to the American constitution in 1791.

Mason was the dominant figure in the committee that framed the Virginia Constitution of 1776, organizing the colony's new statehood, and in 1777 he served for a time on the committee of five Law Revisors which drafted bills—among them Jefferson's Statute of Religious Freedom—giving specific legislative application to the general principles in the declaration of rights.

In 1785, he was a Virginia delegate to the meeting at Mount Vernon whose initial purpose was to consider trade problems of Maryland and Virginia, but whose report on broader matters of defense, finance and tariffs led first to an assembly with wider representation in Annapolis and finally to the convention in Philadelphia that drafted the Federal Constitution.

When this document was prepared in the summer of 1787, Mason was a member of the delegation whose "Virginia Plan" provided the agenda of debate, and Madison's notes show him to have been one of the five most active participants, among the representatives of all the colonies, in the exchange of views that forged the final instrument.

Chiefly because the proposed constitution did not contain a bill of rights, however, when the draft was ready for submission to the states, Mason refused to sign it, and opposed its acceptance as a member of the Virginia ratifying convention the following summer; he was a member of the committee drafting Virginia's proposals for subsequent amendments.

Most of Mason's public writings pertained to issues decided within his lifetime, but throughout his maturity he also expressed himself repeatedly on one that was not settled until seventy years after his death, the issue of slavery. In his first state paper in 1765 he declared that "The policy of encouraging the importation of free people and discouraging that of slaves has never been duly considered in this colony, or we should not at this day see half of our best lands in most parts of the country remain unsettled and the other cultivated with slaves; not to mention the ill effect such a practice has upon the morals and manners of our people." One of his last speeches in the Virginia ratifying convention of 1789 was a denunciation of the clause in the constitution which permitted the importation of slaves to continue for a further twenty years.

But the great documents were not Mason's only anonymous contribution to the life and future of the young republic. Equally important, perhaps, was the impress he left through his personal and private influence on men. A foreign observer, Philip Mazzei, who met Mason just after his arrival in Virginia in 1773, noted in his Memoir: "Among the guests was George Mason, a comrade and intimate friend of George Washington. . . . Mr. Mason made several profound, opportune, and very useful remarks which, by means of the guests— of whom only two were from the same County—were quickly spread through the country, as was every thing else which was said on that subject so interesting to every one."

Gunston Hall is just off the old King's Highway—today's US Route No. 1—its hospitality to neighbors and to travellers along the road on which Mason himself rode south to Williamsburg, north to Philadelphia, included a hospitality of the mind that is recorded in the letters and diaries of most of his great contemporaries.

His two immediate neighbors along the Potomac were Washington at Mount Vernon and, until he returned to England just before the Revolution, George William Fairfax at Belvoir. From the beginning of the crisis in the 1760's until Washington left Virginia to become commander-in-chief, and again after Washington's return from the war until coolness developed during the ratification of the constitution in Virginia, Washington's diaries record their frequent consultation on public questions.

The letters of such contrasting personalities as Richard Henry Lee, Edmund Pendleton, George Rogers Clark, Madison and Monroe substantiate Edmund Randolph's estimate in his History of Virginia: "Among the numbers, who in their small circles were propagating with activity the American doctrines, was George Mason in the shade of retirement. He extended their grasp upon the opinions and affections of those with whom he conversed. How he learned his indifference for distinction, endowed as he was with ability to mount in any line; or whence he contracted his hatred for pomp, with a fortune competent to any expense, and a disposition not adverse from hospitality, can be solved only from that philosophic spirit which despised the adulterated means of cultivating happiness."

Among the four of Mason's Virginia contemporaries who became presidents of the United States, his closest and most sustained relationship was with Jefferson. From the first emergence of the "Movement Party" in the 1760's, they saw events eye to eye for thirty years. Mason's Constitution of Virginia bore a preamble written by Jefferson; Jefferson's Declaration of Independence contracted its phrase, "life, liberty, and the pursuit of happiness" from Mason's Declaration of Rights. During Jefferson's years abroad they maintained an active correspondence; after Mason declined a US Senatorship from Virginia and Jefferson became Secretary of State in Washington's first cabinet, Jefferson wrote: "Certainly whenever I pass your road I shall do myself the pleasure of turning into it." It was on such an occasion, on the last day of September, 1792, that the two passed together at Gunston Hall the final Sunday of George Mason's life.

I

POTOMAC TIDEWATER

George Mason of Gunston Hall was the fourth of his name and line to live in the Northern Neck of Virginia. The first George Mason to come to the colony—he may have inherited his interest from a George Mason who subscribed to the London Company's overseas ventures in 1620—was a Cavalier refugee who emigrated following the defeat of Charles II at the battle of Worcester in 1651. He sailed up Chesapeake Bay and the Potomac from Norfolk, and established himself on an initial grant of 900 acres on the west side of the river; a sixty-mile square, laid on the map of Maryland and Virginia with the river as its diagonal, blocks out the central scene of his activities and those of the next three generations of his descendants.

By the time George Mason of Gunston Hall was born in 1725, the family owned land on both shores of the Potomac, including the sites of several ferries where the King's Highway crossed its tributaries on the Virginia side; the third George Mason made his home on the Maryland side for the five years preceding his death on the river in 1735, when a sudden squall capsized his boat.

Ann Thomson Mason, left a widow with three children—George, ten; Mary, four; and Thomson, two—returned to Virginia to occupy as her dower the plantation at Chappawamsic.

The neighborhood of Chappawamsic, when Mason was growing up, was busy with new activity. To the nearby port of Dumfries came ocean-going sailing ships, bringing household goods, from silver to spinets, table delicacies, men's and women's fashions, and taking abroad timber, furs, grain, and Virginia's all-important staple, tobacco. The merchants of Glasgow, where the tobacco was traded to the Farmers General of France in a row of shops known as Virginia Street, had made George Mason III a freeman of the city, presenting him with a burgess ticket on which a gay red-and-blue coat of arms accompanied the scrolly motto: "Let Glasgow Flourish."

If Dumfries was the largest of the nearby towns, there was also Colchester, just across the ferry north of the family's Occaquan plantation, with its inn known as one of the best stopping places on the King's Highway, a tavern, according to an English visitor later in the century, "where every luxury that money can purchase is to be obtained at first summons; where the richest viands cover the table, and where ice cooled the Madeira that had been thrice across the ocean."

To the south, at the big bend in the Potomac, was the town of Marlborough, where the children's other guardian, John Mercer, lived and guided young George Mason through the latter phases of his education.

When the boys were small, their mother employed a tutor. Later, Mason's younger brother Thomson was sent to England at eighteen to read law at the Middle Temple as his Thomson forebears had done. But there is no evidence that Mason went even as far afield as William and Mary, the college opened at Williamsburg a generation earlier.

The advanced stages of his training were undoubtedly made under the guidance of the man whose library numbered some thousand books on general subjects, ranging from the classical to the contemporary world, and half as many more on law.

At the time of his guardianship, Mercer was particularly well situated to train a young constitutionalist, for he was working on a compilation of the laws of Virginia. He had begun practice upon arrival in the colony in 1726, but the violence of his temper brought him into frequent contempt of court; in the latter 1730's the House of Burgesses disbarred him. For a ten year period he was forced to content himself with a private life—but he used the interval to produce a standard authority for the guidance of county-court magistrates, reviewing all the British law and statutes in force in the colony as well as the acts of the Virginia legislature. Subsequently, the House of Burgesses not only lifted its ban on Mercer's legal practice; it officially adopted his manual.

In 1746, Mason came of age, and shortly thereafter went to live on the Dogue's Neck plantation.

II

GUNSTON HALL

The Mason family Bible witnessed that on Wednesday, April 4, 1750, the Reverend John Moncure, rector of Overwharton Parish, married George Mason and Ann Eilbeck of Mattawoman, Charles County, Maryland. The Mason and Eilbeck families had been neighbors when the two were children. Soon after the wedding, Hesselius painted their portraits; the originals are now lost, but copies, made by Boudet in 1811, hang in Gunston Hall. Ann's likeness bears out Mason's own description of her, written in the family Bible after her death:

She was something taller than the middle size, and elegantly shaped. Her eyes were black, tender and lively; her features regular and delicate; her complexion remarkably fair and fresh. Lilies and roses (almost without a metaphor) were blended there, and a certain inexpressible air of cheerfulness and health. Innocence and sensibility diffused over her countenance formed a face the very reverse of what is generally called masculine.

These portraits hung in their new home, Gunston Hall, when it was completed in 1758. The name had come down through several generations of Mason's maternal ancestry; his grandmother was Mary Fowke of Gunston Hall in Charles County, Maryland, and her grandfather was Gerard Fowke of Gunston Hall in Staffordshire. The habit of naming new homes in America after old ones in England was general among the planters of Virginia Tidewater; Mason's father had conformed to this tradition when he named one of his plantations Hollin Hall after the home of his mother's people near Ripon. But in April 1775 Mason broke the tradition sharply. Hot upon the news of the first revolutionary battle, he christened the plantation which he later gave to his son George in another manner. He called it Lexington.

The builder of Gunston was William Buckland, a skilled craftsman from Oxfordshire whom Mason's brother, Thomson, brought back with him from England under indenture in 1754. Mason was so well satisfied with his work that he recommended him to friends in Annapolis, where, among other important commissions, he built the Matthias Hammond house.

In their main outlines, Buckland's architectural drawings follow the dominant mode: he had in his possession the chief manuals issued by the more prominent architects of England, and suggestions for various parts of the Hammond House are to be found in Robert Adam's "Ruin of the Palace of the Emperor Diocletian," William Kent's "Designs of Inigo Jones," James Gibbs's "Books of Architecture," and Abraham Swan's "British Architecture," while the Chippendale carving in the southwest room at Gunston points to the influence of Sir William Chambers.

Gunston Hall, for all its impressiveness, is really a storey-and-a-half house. On either side of a hall which runs through from the entrance to the garden door are two ground-floor rooms. A central stairway leads to the rooms above, which are lighted by dormer windows deeply recessed in the steep roof, five to a side. In the downstairs rooms, the woodcarving is of great finesse of detail and variety of pattern. The south room of the garden façade has ornate broken pediments above doors, cabinets, fireplace; its door frames are offset to permit covering the pine sheathing with brocade. Its multiplicity of design and ornate mantel give this room somewhat the air of an apprentice pillar,—Gunston was, after all, Buckland's first commission in the New World. The corresponding room on the land entrance side has delicate carvings in the Chinese Chippendale manner. The two rooms opposite, of which the one on the land entrance side served as Mason's study, are separated by a hall leading to the service door; in the yard beyond were kitchen, well and quarters.

In his old age, John Mason, the fourth son in the procession of nine little Masons arriving between 1753 and 1770, wrote a detailed account of the place, both inside and out, as he remembered it from his boyhood. The children's clothes were kept in a chest in his mother's room, with a shirt drawer, a gown drawer, a jacket drawer, and a cap drawer. Mrs. Mason's own clothes were hung in the right-hand closet beside the chimney, and in the same place, hooked to the wall by a silver ring, was a slender green whip, which she took with her when she went riding, but which touched the children more intimately under the name of "the green doctor." The contents of the left-hand closet were so much more sought after that it was known with simple distinctiveness as "the" closet; it contained the smaller delicacies that enriched the family table.

To the west of the main building was the schoolhouse—most of the children were educated at home as their father had been. Beyond the schoolhouse, blocked off from view by walnut trees, were stables for all the horses except the stud stallion, Vulcan, kept in isolation behind the high bars of a paddock next to the orchard. Beyond the stables, on the edge of the woods, was "Log Town," made up of the pine log-cabins of the plantation slaves.

The last twelve hundred feet of the connecting road which led in to Gunston's from the main north-south highway were flanked on each side by two rows of black heart cherry trees, grown from seed for the sake of uniformity.

When standing at this western entrance the visitor who arrived on horseback or by carriage could look through and see, framed by the door at the opposite end of the hall, the first vistas of the formal garden south of the house. In order to get the flat area required for its geometric patterns, Mason graded the top of the hill. He bordered the central walk with box hedges which today, grown to twice the height of a man, are still in their original place. Here were planted a variety of flowers—Persian jessamine, guelder-rose—whose cuttings Mason sent, from time to time, as gifts to the Washington garden at Mount Vernon. Some two hundred feet from the house the land falls off sharply to a plain on the level of the river which was grazed by a domesticated herd of deer from the surrounding woodlands. Skirting the park, a road descended from the kitchen yard to the river landing, where crops were loaded in scows for transshipment to ocean-going vessels, and where the small craft used for fishing and hunting were kept. To the north of the landing was the orchard, as much an object of Mason's pride and generosity as his garden. Washington's diary for the 1760's records a long series of plantings of fruit from Gunston.

The intensive cultivation around the house was only the focal point of the plantation culture. In the near vicinity lay five thousand acres of fields and woods, on whose produce the concentrated domestic well-being depended. Four different areas within this tract were worked by groups of slaves under an overseer; they raised a certain amount of corn for home consumption, but the chief crops were tobacco and wheat for sale. Mason managed the establishment himself, without the aid of a steward, and attended to the insurance, shipment, and marketing of the tobacco and other products that he sold abroad.

The Mason's nearest neighbors were the Cockburns of Springfield; after Mrs. Mason's death, they took charge of the household during Mason's absences. Somewhat further afield were the homes of Mason's sister and various families of cousins, the Blackburns at Ripon Lodge, the McCartys at Cedar Grove.

From one of these households to another circled the leisurely currents of plantation life. George Washington's diary for 1770 notes that on April 18 "Patcy Custis and Milly Posey went to Col° Mason's to the Dancing School." There were balls at Alexandria; at the Dumfries theater "The Recruiting Officer" was playing in February 1771 when Mason and Washington went down to arbitrate a case in which Mercer and Thomson Mason were the lawyers. There was the race track at Bogges's near Pohick, in the midst of whose gay confusion at five o'clock of the afternoon of May 6, 1758, Mason scribbled a note recommending his cousin French Mason to Washington for a commission in the army.

In his early teens Washington, seven years younger than Mason, had stayed frequently at Mount Vernon while it still belonged to Lawrence, his half-brother and guardian; Mason came to near-by Dogue's Neck when he was twenty-one. From then on, until Washington left Virginia to lead the American army, they were constantly together, appearing occasionally as public figures, continually as private gentlemen.

During the war the two kept up a scattered correspondence; a letter of one of the Lewises of Fredericksburg describes Mason greeting the returned General in 1784:

I must tell you what a charming day I spent at Mount Vernon with Mama and Sally. The general and madame came home on Christmas Eve, and such a racket the servants made, for they were glad of their coming! . . . . Among the most notable of the callers was Mr. George Mason, of Gunston Hall, who was on his way home from Alexandria, and who brought a charming granddaughter with him, about fourteen years old. He is said to be one of the greatest statesmen and wisest men in Virginia. We had heard much of him and were delighted to look in his face, hear him speak, and take his hand, which he offered in a courtly manner. He is straight in figure but not tall, and has a grand head and clear gray eyes. He has few white hairs, though they say he is about sixty years old.

Mason's health was chronically bad; the attack of "convulsive cholic" which caused his death was a last manifestation of a disease which in various forms plagued him, his brother, and his eldest son. Yet it seems doubtful that health was more than a secondary consideration in his lifelong reluctance to serve in public office; there were two other matters which certainly had far more to do with it.

Before the Revolutionary crisis ended petty place-seeking, the Virginia House of Burgesses was a reflection in miniature of the cliques and cabals of the British Parliament; one term in this assembly disgusted Mason and made him warn his sons against the shams of political life.

But what kept him at Gunston more than his compatriots liked after the outbreak of the Revolution was his added responsibility at home following the death of Mrs. Mason early in 1773. Her son John later wrote:

"I remember well her funeral, that the whole family went into deep mourning suddenly prepared, that I was led clothed in black to her grave, that I saw her coffin lowered down into it by cords covered with black cloth, and that there was a large assemblage of friends and neighbors of every class and of the slaves of the estate present; that the house was in a state of desolation for a good while, that the children and servants passed each other in tears and silence or spoke in whispers, and that my father for some days paced the rooms, or from the house to the grave (it was not far) alone."

Mason ordered this inscription on the tombstone that marks her grave in the Gunston Hall burial ground:

Ann Mason, Daughter of William Eilbeck of Charles County in Maryland Merchant, departed this Life on the 9th Day of March 1773 in the 39th Year of her Age, after a long & painful illness, which She bore with uncommon Fortitude & Resignation.

Once She was all that cheers and sweetens Life,
The tender Mother, Daughter, friend and Wife,
Once She was all that makes Mankind adore;
Now view this Marble and be vain no more.

Eleven days later, he made his own will. Its finality gives the impression that his life was nearly over, instead of being on the brink of the events which gave it historical significance. But it is true that its course was very materially changed. His eldest child was just twenty, his youngest, only three. Long absences from home became impracticable. His scruples about going as far as Williamsburg and Richmond were subsequently overcome, but the Convention which framed the Federal Constitution was the only national assembly in whose deliberations he ever shared, and that was after his second marriage, in 1780, to Sarah Brent. Over and over, when a delegation was being selected to represent Virginia in the Continental Congress, he was subjected to strong pressure by his colleagues, but insisted that his first responsibility was at home; the Convention of 1775 refused to allow his name to be dropped until he had risen and explained his position before the entire House; when he resumed his seat there was a silence, and the eyes of Peyton Randolph, the Speaker, were seen to be filled with tears.

Between the duties, pleasures, and routine of his private and domestic life Mason's periods of public service, in the wider sense of service to colony, state, or nation, came like brilliant interludes. By contrast, his service to his immediate community was a consistently continued thing. As town trustee, he fostered the development of Alexandria. As gentleman justice, he helped to administer his county. As vestryman, he brought his influence to bear upon the program of his parish. Out of this constant experience of the problems of local government grew the ideas and policies which he subsequently expressed in more developed detail for jurisdictions of larger scope. The significance of his later work can be fully understood only when he has been seen against the background of his local habitation, in the activities of his neighboring town, his county court, his parish church.

III

ALEXANDRIA

The town of Alexandria, about fifteen miles north of Gunston Hall, was begun in mid-century as a port for overseas shipments. The nearby area had been bought at the end of the seventeenth century by Robert Alexander for one pound of tobacco per acre; a hamlet had existed from the time of the erection of a government tobacco warehouse in 1732; in 1748 Lawrence Washington, newly elected burgess from the district, secured from the Assembly the necessary legislation for the establishment of the town. On June 13, 1749, ten streets were laid off and sixty-seven lots offered at public auction.

In 1754 a building for the county court was put up on one side of the market square; on court days the auctioning of the tax tobacco gathered a crowd around the courthouse door, as well as the execution of court judgments prescribing the pillory or the whipping post. The green in front of the courthouse was also used as a drill ground; Washington collected recruits for his expedition to Great Meadows there, and it was there that the band played "The Girl I Left Behind Me" as Braddock's men started west two years later. At the outbreak of the Revolution it became the parade ground of the Independent Blues.

In 1754 George Mason was appointed to Alexandria's Board of Trustees to succeed Philip Alexander, deceased. Two years earlier, Lawrence Washington's place had been taken by George Johnston; when it again fell vacant in 1766, George Washington was the unanimous choice. Both served until the town was incorporated in 1779. Most of the trustees who lived any distance from Alexandria built offices there where they transacted their public business or spent the night when delayed by public meetings. Mason's office was on the corner of King and Royal streets, Washington's on Cameron.

Market and court days, local festivities, and through travel from colony to colony created a demand for transient accommodations in Alexandria. There were taverns to suit the taste and purse of all sorts and conditions of men. The most famous was Gadsby's. Washington made it his headquarters in 1754; from its doorstep he gave his last order to the Independent Blues; he was present when Virginia's adoption of the Constitution was celebrated; and he was publicly honored there by the first Washington's Birthnight Ball. In the coachyard back of the Inn, in 1777, Lafayette and Baron de Kalb were found struggling alike with the English language and the man in charge of their horses, and were aided by a young sailor called John Paul Jones.

Two important churches were put up before the Revolution. Christ Church was completed in 1773; the first Presbyterian meeting house in 1774. Besides the established churches, several sects of Dissenters were active in the town. The Methodists met in an old sail loft near the river front; they were occasionally led by Frances Asbury, the first American bishop, whom the Wesleys sent over in 1771. The law required Dissenters to obtain licenses both for their preachers and for their meeting places: among the ministers arrested for non-compliance, Jeremiah Moore was jailed in Alexandria.

By coincidence, Alexandria was the place where first was formulated the British tax policy against which the colonies rose. In the spring of 1755, General Braddock arrived with his royal troops and a British fleet and spent some weeks there prior to the western campaign that marked the official beginning of the French and Indian War. As part of his preparation he called a meeting of royal governors, Shirley of Massachusetts, De Lancey of New York, Sharpe of Maryland, Morris of Pennsylvania, and Dinwiddie of Virginia. They met in the Blue Room of the Carlyle House, and deliberated on plans of campaign and ways and means of meeting the cost of the war. Shirley suggested a tax on the colonists, and Braddock promptly referred to his superiors the idea "of laying a tax upon all His Majesty's dominions in America, agreeably to the result of council, for reimbursing the great sums that must be advanced for the service and interest of the colonies in this important crisis." Ten years later, when the time came to pay for the war, Shirley's suggestion was adopted, the Stamp Act was passed, and "taxation without representation" became fighting words.

IV

FAIRFAX COURT

Meetings of the Alexandria trustees were not the only meetings which brought such men as Mason and Washington to town. Alexandria was then also the seat of government of Fairfax County, and many of the town trustees presided over this larger jurisdiction in the capacity of gentlemen justices.

The court served as executive, judiciary, and legislature. People of all degrees gathered at its monthly sessions, from the river plantations and from the upland farms; the meetings gave cohesion to a scattered agricultural population and made possible the development of a public opinion. And because America as a whole was preponderantly agricultural, the problems and progress of the local community constituted a model of the problems and progress of the larger area of colony and confederation of colonies. All up and down the coast, at the beginning of the second half of the eighteenth century, the men who later hammered out the political theory of American statehood were practically without exception acquiring the basis for their proposals in experience of the homely, concrete, local case.

In the pre-Revolutionary years, the gentlemen justices of Fairfax Court had, at times, the Lord Proprietor of the Northern Neck himself as their presiding personage; for several months during various winters Lord Fairfax left Greenway Court, his estate near Winchester, and traveled up to town accompanied by his cousin, Bryan Fairfax, later rector of Christ Church, Alexandria, and successor to the Fairfax title. Among the other justices were William Ramsay, George Washington, George Mason, G. W. Fairfax, John Carlyle.

The variety of subjects which claimed Mason's attention as gentleman justice can be read in the agenda of the court's monthly meetings.

There were three classes of business—the executive and administrative affairs of the community, the prosecutions brought in the interest of the public on the basis of grand jury indictments, and the lawsuits between private parties.

The court had charge of county taxation. It prepared the lists of tithables that were used alike for civil and church levies; and since the assessments were levied in pounds of tobacco, it erected a series of storage warehouses. The amount of the civil levy varied somewhat with the years in proportion to the current public works program, but in general it ran from ten to fifteen pounds of tobacco per taxpayer, giving the court an annual revenue of from twenty to thirty thousand pounds.

The rate of exchange between tobacco and currency was regulated periodically, debts on one occasion being payable in "money or to-bacco at the rate of 12/6 per C^r, and that they do not presume to de-mand more of any person whatsoever." Inns and ordinaries were licensed; their keepers bonded for good behavior; and the rates they might charge their guests set annually. In 1760:

For a night's lodging with clean sheets .... 6^d
Otherwise nothing
All soldiers and expresses on his Majesty's service paying ready mony shall have one fifth part deducted
For a hot dyet .... 9^d
With small beer or cyder 1/0
For a cold dyet .... 6^d
With small beer or cyder .... 9^d

The condition of the roads, bridges and ferries, as well as the inns was watched over by the court; it was out of the tithe tobacco that George Mason's annual two thousand pounds for keeping Occaquan ferry came.

Among the court's administrative functions was the registration of valuable papers, army and other commissions, leases, deeds, wills, inventories and appraisals (among these are frequent estimates of the age of negroes). Marriage contracts are numerous, registering prenuptial agreements as to the disposal of the partners' worldly goods; typical is the contract between George Mason and his second wife, Sarah Brent, by which he was to have the use of her slaves during his lifetime and she to get them back together with a certain number of acres of land for her dower right after his death.

The court was also charged with the giving of oaths of office. Before a man could serve as a justice, sheriff, vestryman, or attorney, he had to subscribe to the Test Acts, witnessing his allegiance to the

King and Church of England; Roman Catholics were prevented from participating in public office by the clause, "I do declare that there is no Transsubstantiation in the Sacrament of the Lord's Supper or in the Elements of Bread and Wine at or after the Consecration Thereof by any person Whatsoever."

When acting on presentments by the grand jury, the court collaborated closely with the vestry, for the presentments frequently had to do with morals, and were brought at the instance of the churchwardens. The grand jury presented "John Cockrill of Truro Parish for not attending his Parish Church within two months last past to the knowledge of two of us;" it called Edward Violett to account "for keeping a disorderly house on the Sabbath day," and William Carter "for breach of the Sabbath by employing two negroes about working his tobacco ground." William Ferguson was had up, "for prophanely swearing, by his God, five times in the parish and county, aforesaid, to the knowledge of two of us"; Richard Morris was charged with being drunk, Jane Morrison with having a baseborn child, Harniss Jenkins as an idle vagrant.

While no formal impediment to the trial of serious cases by the county courts existed, a practically unbroken precedent of dealing with such matters at Williamsburg had resulted from the establishment of a General Court at the capital some years before the creation of local tribunals. By consequence, in the early Fairfax Court minute books only one hanging is recorded.

In the ordinary course of affairs, the private cases brought before the court were cases involving breaches of the peace, and cases involving money. The common way of dealing with debtors was imprisonment. In October, 1770, the case of Mason v. Sewell was decided against the latter. Sewell was imprisoned for the customary twenty days; at the end of the time he delivered a schedule of his entire estate:

"1 flock bed, 2 blankets, 1 rug, 1 hog, 1 gun, 2 plates, 1 bason, 1 iron pott, some earthenware, 1 chest, some pewter spoons, 5/—owing from William Ferguson, 1 water pail, 1 frying pan, 1 pair forks, 2 or 3 old knives and forks, 2 rugs, 1 pair horse fleems."

After these goods were sold for 21/3, Sewell was released.

V

Truro Vestry

English law, which the colonists brought with them for the governance of Virginia, included not only civil law but canon law, establishing the Church of England, in which the Virginia churches were grouped under the diocese of London. The vestries of the Virginia churches shared with the county courts responsibility for local government; the latter, on the basis of the county, dealt with the legal relations of the community; the former, on the basis of the parish, cared for its moral and charitable obligations.

The Parish of Truro, covering the territory in the Northern Neck north of Occaquan Creek, was created by an Act of the Assembly in 1732. The number of tithable parishioners in that year was 676; in the course of a generation it mounted rapidly to some fourteen hundred. The tithes assessed upon them by the vestry—whose members, as in the case of Mason and Washington, were often justices of the court as well—also showed a tendency to mount; in the years just preceding the Revolution, the Truro vestry disposed of an annual sum of approximately thirty-eight thousand pounds.

The portion that was spent for the poor was mostly given to various householders in the parish for the support of homeless children, old people, or dependents, and often included burial expenses later; as the children grew older, the vestry apprenticed them to a trade. Beginning about 1745 the first steps toward a public health service were made as the vestry began payments to the doctors in the various settlements, amounting to about twelve hundred pounds apiece a year, for tending the poor. Employment of the able-bodied poor was a further task; in 1775 a committee was appointed with Mason as one of its members to prepare a plan. At times of crisis and crop failure, out-and-out relief was requisite.

At the end of the seventeenth century the Virginia churches revived the old English custom of "walking the bounds." Every four years, the boundaries of all the lands in the parish were gone over in official procession, to minimize boundary disputes by keeping the lines fresh in mind.

Such was the business of the vestry in so far as it was concerned with works. Another series of activities expressed its concern with faith. One of its problems was to find and maintain a minister; after a series of difficulties, a neighborhood lawyer, Lee Massey, was prevailed on to take orders; he served the parish from 1766 until after the Revolution.

The vestry was also responsible for providing suitable places of worship and a glebe for the minister. In 1752 a contract for a new glebe, to be made of brick, was awarded. After some exasperating delays, in 1758 the remainder of the work was given a more satisfactory craftsman, William Buckland, who had just completed Mason's Gunston Hall.

In 1765, Truro was divided into two parishes, Truro and Fairfax; George Washington's lands, according to the first allotment by the Assembly, fell in the new parish, but were restored to Truro by an amendment the following spring. Washington kept a record of the votes in the ensuing election of vestrymen; the three highest were George Mason, 282; Edward Payne, 277; George Washington, 259.

With Payne as the contractor, a brick church was then undertaken in the western part of the parish and while it was yet uncompleted, a still more elaborate program was adopted for the building of New Pohick.

The selection of the site for this church was the occasion of a difference between George Mason and George Washington. Mason urged that the new church be built on the old site, out of respect for Old Pohick's tradition; Washington urged a new site, on the grounds of greater convenience to the parishioners. The proposed new site was not far from Mount Vernon; the site of Old Pohick not far from Gunston Hall. On the day the final decision was reached, every member of the vestry was present, and Washington carried his point by exhibiting a spot survey of the parish, showing that Old Pohick was far removed from the center of population. The Vestry Book succinctly records: "Resolved, that a church be built at or as near the cross road leading from Hollis's to Pohick warehouse as water can be had, which resolution was carried by a majority of 7 to 5." But George Mason was closely concerned with the building of New Pohick. The contract was let in March, 1769, to a vestryman who began the structure but shortly died; as his executor, Mason completed the work. There is great similarity in design between the ornamental woodwork of Pohick Church and some of that of Gunston Hall.

By midwinter of 1773 the last of the interior finish was completed. On February 15, 1774, the church was formally received from George Mason with the understanding that he should "finish the horse blocks and benches under the trees."

VI

WESTERN VENTURES

The training in public affairs which Mason received through familiarity with the public life of his locality was supplemented by one other important connection. Few men in America at the outbreak of the Revolution knew both the settled part of the country and the frontier. But because of his association with the Ohio Company, Mason was one of them.

The Ohio Company was organized in 1748, to open up and settle the western lands within the chartered limits of Virginia and to compete with the Pennsylvanians for trade with the Indians. Its stockholders shortly included, besides Virginia's Governor Dinwiddie and Thomas Ludwell Lee, who was chairman, Washington's half-brother Lawrence, who succeeded to the chairmanship on the death of Lee, Mason's former guardian, John Mercer, who became secretary, and Mason, who over a long period was treasurer.

The 500,000 acres of Virginia's western territory granted to the Ohio Company by the Lords of Trade formed a rough triangle, with its apex at the site of present-day Pittsburgh, its western leg traced by the Ohio River, and its eastern leg sighted from Pittsburgh through the headwaters of the Potomac to the headwaters of the James. On the upper 200,000 acres of this land, the company undertook to carry out its projects, and set in motion a series of political events in which the future of continents was involved. The European struggle for world empire, in which England defeated France between 1750 and 1763, had fronts in both the Orient and the New World; and in East and West alike it was the penetration of a British trading company into French-claimed territory that precipitated the military engagement.

The implications of the Ohio Company's activities were at first unperceived. Mason's early association, like that of its other members, was purely speculative. Christopher Gist, a frontiersman who was probably the first white settler west of the Alleghenies, made two journeys of reconnaissance; the accounts he brought back formed a flavorful prospectus. Yet development was repeatedly deferred. The company erected a warehouse some two hundred miles up the Potomac from Alexandria, and filled it with £4000 worth of goods from London for the Indian trade, but the traders complained that the absence of a road to the West reduced profits to a vanishing point. Lawrence Washington interested a group of German and Pennsylvania Dutch emigrants, but Governor Dinwiddie's dalliance in assuring them a preliminary period of parish tax exemption cooled their enthusiasm. Again, when work was begun on the fort whose erection was one of the conditions of the company's grant, the Pennsylvanians objected to the site; jealousy between Pennsylvanians and Virginians had an economic foundation in competition for the Indian trade, and a political one in their common boundary, unsettled until Mason and Dixon's survey in 1763-1767.

More far-reaching was the political dispute between Virginia and the royal authority as to whether the Indian treaties had vested title to the western territories in the colony or in the crown. On either basis, the British claims were disputed by the Indians and the French.

The Indians denied that they had ever ceded jurisdiction over the area contained in the Company's grant. In 1752 a partial cession, covering only the lands southeast of the Ohio, was obtained from them through the mediation of Christopher Gist, but was revoked the following year. After that they were the ready allies of whatever authority attempted to hold back the Virginians.

They were soon called upon by the French, who had formally proclaimed their sovereignty over the entire area from the Great Lakes to the Ohio River between the mountains and the Mississippi and moved to secure its eastern boundary.

The first actual clash occurred when the French drove off Virginia workmen building a fort at the site of present-day Pittsburgh, completed it themselves and named it Fort Duquesne. At the end of 1753, Virginia's Governor Dinwiddie sent one of his young colonels, George Washington, with a warning to the French commandant to retire; the following year, as the commandant remained firm, the Governor followed up his warning by an expedition, of which Washington eventually had command, to retake the captured fort. After several preliminary skirmishes, Washington was forced to surrender a hastily built shelter near Great Meadows which he had named Fort Necessity and lead his troops back to eastern Virginia. News of the defeat was carried to England, where the incident became a matter of Empire prestige. A general attack on the French strongholds in the New World was mapped out; Braddock was dispatched to Alexandria to initiate the capture of Fort Duquesne; the French and Indian War had begun.

At the end of 1761, the Lords of Trade sent instructions to the colonial governors forbidding them to make any grants of lands in the West; in 1763 a royal proclamation declared the landward boundary of the thirteen colonies to be the Allegheny watershed, ordered all settlers beyond that limit to withdraw, and set aside the Northwest Territory for an Indian reservation. And though Burke fulminated that this was "an attempt to keep as a lair of wild beasts that earth which God, by an express charter, has given to the children of men," the proclamation stood.

Then a company of Pennsylvanians conceived a plan for a colonizing enterprise at the expense of the Virginians. According to the new proclamation, the territory of the original colonies stopped at the watershed; the new Indian reservation went no further south than the Ohio River. Under such premises, the land south of the river and west of Virginia was the direct property of the crown. In 1772, some American promotors, including Benjamin Franklin and Samuel Wharton, were empowered to form the Grand Company.

At that time, the Ohio Company's agent in London was Mason's cousin, John Mercer's son George. The organizers of the Grand Company offered him two of the seventy-two shares of the Grand Company's stock in return for the Ohio Company's entire interest in the western territory, and one share in return for his own, and whispered in his ear that the governorship of the new province might possibly come his way. He agreed.

When the news reached Virginia, the members of the Ohio Company determined not only to repudiate their agent's act, but to set forth a detailed statement of their case against the crown for chartering the Grand Company. George Mason was charged with the compilation of this document.

Mason prepared his "Extracts from the Virginia Charters With Some Remarks upon Them" to clarify the circumstances of a particular case, but in doing so he advanced principles applicable to far wider issues. His initial purpose was to refute Franklin's contention that the crown was justified in disposing of the disputed area. But when presented to the Virginia Assembly of 1773, his demonstration that the early Virginia charters had deeded all of the Northwest Territory to Virginia planted in the minds of her citizens a conviction that their boundaries stopped only on the shores of the Great Lakes. Thenceforth the crest of the Alleghenies became the same kind of strategic frontier between England and Virginia as it had been between England and France.

VII

WILLIAMSBURG

The tension which began in the 1760's called Mason from the affairs of his locality into the larger life of the colony. He was continually asked to draft statements of policy, and time after time the documents which he prepared were passed on from one governmental organ to another of larger jurisdiction until they became the expression of the newly forming continental point of view.

Mason's early political visits to Williamsburg were for meetings of the Ohio Company or the Assembly. The town presented an appearance unique among colonial capitals. Except as a center of government, its existence was negligible. Virginia's four great rivers, the James, the York, the Rappahannock and the Potomac, provided a system of inland waterways that enabled the planters to trade directly abroad; as a result, Virginia developed no mercantile class and no commercial capital comparable in wealth and influence to Charleston, Philadelphia, New York or Boston. Williamsburg was a place of seasons: during sessions of the House of Burgesses, the general court, or the governor's council, it was packed with persons and personages drawn together by the demands and opportunities of politics, society, and litigation; at other times it relapsed into a quiet so deep that the dust of Duke of Gloucester Street was hardly troubled by a passing hoof. The only public buildings with more or less permanent occupants were the Governor's Palace, the College of William and Mary, the lunatic asylum, and the jail. For two thirds of every year, the arched brick colonnades of the state house, styled "The Capitol" in the full tide of classic revival, were empty of footsteps; the Raleigh Tavern had ample space for the traveler; the theater was dark; weeds grew in the race track on the edge of town. Transitory residence was reflected in the domestic architecture; a few brick houses and several clapboard ones of considerable proportions indicated the eight or ten families of importance who made the capital their permanent home, but the typical house was a storey-and-a-half white frame structure of simple design, occupied by one of the great plantation households for a few weeks several times in the course of the year.

Once the season was on, however, Williamsburg quickened with a gaiety proportionate to the preceding calm. At the race track, the light glinted on the polished thoroughbreds of Colonel Byrd and Colonel Tayloe. The latest successes from London entranced the playgoer. Boys ran down the streets with fresh copies of the *Virginia Gazette*. Taproom patrons of the Raleigh Tavern called for Harry Wetherburn's biggest bowl of arrack punch; in some of the smaller rooms the gaming fever the colony had caught from winsome Governor Francis Fauquier distributed gains and losses which for most people averaged more than the modest sums carefully entered in Washington's daybook. The Apollo Room was reserved far ahead for the balls about which the daughters of the river plantations were chattering. Interspersed with such social gaiety, the not-too-pressing business of the colony was carried forward.

The forms of eighteenth-century life, as they had developed by 1755, continued in the colonial capital for twenty years. Up to the last moment before separation there were no riotous incidents in Virginia as there had been in Massachusetts; even after the break the groundwork of the new political structure varied little from the old. The legislative and judicial branches of government had always been composed exclusively of citizens of the colony; in the sometimes prolonged periods between governors the President of the Council had taken the executive's place. Even in the matter of defense, the French and Indian War had disclosed the colony's indigenous leadership in Washington. With remarkably few alterations, the machinery which had served the colony served the commonwealth; with equally few changes the men who had made the colony were the men who made the new state. The revolution was a revolution in the ideas of those men.

These ideas developed from specific cases. As early as 1753, an extra unauthorized fee of one pistole was laid on the issuance of titles by the land office. Western settlers complained. The Burgesses instructed the Attorney-General to go abroad to obtain redress. In his pamphlet, "Fragment on the Pistole Fee," Richard Bland said that there is no assurance that a power which will impose a fee of one pistole will not impose a fee of a hundred; he compared liberty and property to precious vessels whose value is destroyed by the slightest hole. The sending of the Attorney-General was the first step in direct representation of the Burgesses at London. After the Two Penny Act and the Parsons Cause they maintained a permanent agent there.

The Parsons Cause had its origin in the colony's use of tobacco as currency in the payment of all debts, fees, stipends, and so forth. At the end of the fifties an acute shortage in the tobacco crop, persisting over several years, sent tobacco prices soaring. The Assembly provided relief for the planters by passing the Two Penny Act. This permitted settlement of obligations that were normally paid in tobacco in currency at an exchange rate of twopence per pound. Among the salaries affected were those of the Church of England ministers; they obtained a royal disallowance of the Act, and brought suit against their vestries for damages. Patrick Henry, defending the vestrymen, charged the parsons with profiteering, and swayed the jury into allowing them a penny for their pains.

Then the passage of the Stamp Act brought on the first real crisis. The Seven Years' War had to be paid for; in the spring of 1764 Parliament, after levying duties on colonial imports of Madeira wine and a series of other goods, suggested the desirability of a tax on the stamps used on legal papers. The Virginia Assembly immediately drew up a case against such taxation for use by its London agent. When the Burgesses met again in October, they had before them the remonstrance of the Massachusetts House; thus strengthened, they prepared memorials to the Crown, the Lords, the Commons, pointing to Virginia's charter rights to internal self-government. The following spring, however, the Stamp Act was voted.

The news of its passage galvanized the colony. The Assembly adopted a series of resolutions by Patrick Henry, of which the fifth and most outspoken read:

Resolved that the General Assembly of this colony have the sole right and power to lay taxes and impositions on the inhabitants of this colony, and that every attempt to vest such power in any person or persons whatsoever other than the General Assembly afores^d has a manifest tendency to destroy British as well as American freedom.

The phraseology of this statement differed so radically from the conciliatory terms used in past memorials that members of the House older and more experienced than the newly elected Henry opposed it; it passed only by a single vote and two days later it was deleted from the record. But the text was nevertheless circulated through the other colonies, and did much to consolidate the united opposition recorded by the Stamp Act Congress in Albany in October.

Meanwhile in Westmoreland County, Richard Henry Lee prepared a statement on the basis of which the justices announced themselves unable to serve under the new law. The Stafford court resigned in a body. Washington and George William Fairfax, the burgesses from Fairfax County, asked Mason to draw up a scheme for replevying goods under distress for rent which would avoid the use of stamped paper while permitting the landlord to recover in case of continued nonpayment.

Because the *Virginia Gazette* was regarded as too much under administration influence, a rival paper was established in Williamsburg to publish articles on the new issues. Richard Bland wrote his "Inquiry into the Rights of the British Colonies," carrying on from the familiar negative statement, that the colonies are not subject to internal legislation passed by a nonrepresentative Parliament, to the conclusion that the colonies are united to England only through the crown.

Tension was mounting rapidly when control of the British government passed from Grenville to Rockingham and the Stamp Act was suddenly repealed. The scenes of jubilation which took place at the Raleigh on arrival of the news were duplicated in every colony along the coast; an era of good feeling followed.

Immediate grievances were put away, yet fundamental differences remained unresolved. A committee of London merchants published an open letter to the colonists, calling upon them to be grateful for the concession. In reply, dated June 6, 1766, signed " A Virginia Planter," and printed in the London *Public Ledger,* Mason made a spirited statement of the colonists' prevailing mood: they were ready wholeheartedly to welcome the repeal as an act of justice; that it was a favor, they would never admit. The combined loyalty and independence expressed in Mason's letter were representative of the vast majority of his fellow Virginians. The former accounted for the tranquillity of the year 1766. The latter set the streets of Williamsburg again buzzing with excitement when, in 1767, word arrived of the passage of the Townshend Acts, by which, among other things, new duties were laid on glass, on painters' colors, on paper, and on tea.

VIII

THE INTERRUPTION OF TRADE

The news of the Townshend duties raised again the issues which had lately been quiescent. In February, 1768, Massachusetts sent out a circular letter inviting concerted protests. In an effort to break the united front that was developing, the ministry at Whitehall adopted diametrically opposite methods of treatment for Massachusetts and Virginia: force in the North, flattery in the South. A British garrison was dispatched to occupy Boston; His Excellency, the Right Honourable Norborne Berkeley, Baron de Botetourt, was appointed governor of Virginia.

His Lordship did things in the grand manner: under his direction the convocation of the Assembly in May, 1769, imitated the ceremony of a parliamentary opening at Westminster. Attired in a red velvet coat trimmed with gold thread, he drove from the Governor's Palace to the Capitol in a state coach brought from London and drawn by six white horses.

But the members of the Assembly did not allow the great personal popularity of the Governor to interfere with their agenda. During the winter, an obsolete statute had been revived providing for the transportation to England for trial of Americans accused of treason. Six days after the session opened, the Burgesses prepared a memorial in which they announced that

we cannot, without horror, think of the new, unusual, & permit us with all humility to add, unconstitutional & illegal mode recommended to your Majesty, of seizing & carrying beyond sea, the inhabitants of America suspected of any crime.

When the Governor heard of this action he summoned the Burgesses to the council chamber. As the Speaker faced him, he said: "Gentlemen, I have heard of your resolves and augur ill of their effect. You have made it my duty to dissolve you, and you are dissolved accordingly."

The dissolution, in any but the legal sense, did not take place. The burgesses continued their deliberations privately. Throughout the spring, consultations between members of the House had been in progress as to an effective method of expressing their dissatisfaction with the new duties. Washington had written Mason April 5, 1769, asking for his opinion and saying that arms should be their last resort;—since addresses to the throne had proved futile, how about starving trade? Mason replied the same day that while no plan could be adopted before the meeting of the Assembly, something should be published at once in the various news sheets to prepare the public mind; he had such an article under way. As an upshot of this exchange, when Washington went to Williamsburg he had a set of draft resolutions in his pocket. The prorogued burgesses adopted those stipulating that no goods should be purchased overseas and formed a non-importation association.

Soon thereafter, at one of Lord Botetourt's balls, over a hundred of the ladies present were dressed in homespun; William Nelson, President of the Council, proudly wrote to a merchant friend in London that his suit and shirts, his shoes, hose, buckles, wig, and hat, were all made in his own country. Confident that something had been accomplished, the burgesses at the November Assembly received with applause the governor's speech promising satisfaction to the colonies.

In April, 1770, the Townshend duties were repealed, but an exception, by the King's will, was made of tea. As a result, the production of revenue was abandoned while the question of principle was surrounded with the psychology of a test case.

Yet the colonial boycott was only partially successful; in December Mason wrote a relative in England doubting whether real effectiveness could be obtained without the adoption of a single uniform scheme by all the colonies. He hoped that repeal would lay the matter at rest before such a measure had to be taken, yet he prepared to press on in its absence:

There are not five men of sense in America who would accept of independence if it was offered; we know that our own happiness, our very being depends upon our being connected with our Mother Country . . . but we will not submit to have our own money taken out of our pockets without our consent, because if any man or any set of men take from us without our consent or that of our representatives one shilling in the pound we have no security for the remaining nineteen. We owe our Mother Country the duty of subjects; we will not pay her the submission of slaves.

For the next four years relations gradually worsened. Lord Botetourt died, and was replaced by Lord Dunmore, who in all phases of his administration was as unpopular as his predecessor had been successful.

In January, 1773, Samuel Adams sent Richard Henry Lee the procedures by which committees of correspondence were being organized in the Massachusetts towns; shortly, similar committees were established all along the coast.

Late that autumn a fleet of tea ships was dispatched to the four chief American ports. At Charleston, the tea was debarked but left to mold in a damp basement. At Philadelphia, the inhabitants persuaded the ship's captain to return with his cargo unlanded. The New York ships were driven off by a gale. The Boston Tea Party took place on December 16.

For the next five months the appearance of outward calm thinly covered a revived tension. Little by little, word-of-mouth communication from county to county and colony to colony brought into being a sense of continental unity. Numerous letters show Mason's part in the creation of this sense in Virginia.

Then, in May, 1774, the suspense as to the results of the Boston Tea Party was broken; news came of the passage of a Port Act, closing Boston to commerce, to take effect on the first of June. The spring Assembly was in session; Mason was not a member but was in Williamsburg on business; he described the burgesses' temper in a letter to Martin Cockburn:

A dissolution . . . is generally expected; but I think will not happen before the house has gone through the public business, which will be late in June.

Whatever resolves or measures are intended for the preservation of our rights and liberties, will be reserved for the conclusion of the session. Matters of that sort here are conducted and prepared with a great deal of privacy, and by very few members; of whom Patrick Henry is the principal. At the request of the gentlemen concerned, I have spent an evening with them upon the subject, where I had an opportunity of conversing with Mr. Henry, and knowing his sentiments; as well as hearing him speak in the house since, on different occasions. He is by far the most powerful speaker I ever heard.

The dissolution which Mason anticipated for June actually occurred later in the day on which he wrote this letter. As in the similar case five years before, the prorogued burgesses continued their business. Reassembled at the Raleigh, they declared that the Boston Act enslaved them, instructed the Committee of Correspondence to sound out the other colonies regarding a Continental Congress; and called a convention to meet on August 1.

IX

THE TURN TOWARD INDEPENDENCE

The eight weeks between the dissolution of the Assembly and the opening of the August convention were spent by the group of men who came to be known as the "Movement Party" in an intensive campaign consolidating and securing an expression of county opinion; practically all of the Virginia counties took some form of corporate action.

In Fairfax, a subscription to aid Boston was opened by Washington and Mason, and on July 18, a county meeting under Washington's chairmanship adopted a series of resolutions, written and read by Mason, and thenceforth known as the Fairfax Resolves. They constitute perhaps the most important pre-Revolutionary document prepared in Virginia.

The Resolves begin with a review of the political theory of the dispute, announcing that the relation of the people of Virginia to the crown is the same as that of the people of Great Britain. Parliament's present membership is incapable of dealing adequately with American affairs. For a considerable period, Parliament has passed, and the American people have accepted, certain regulations covering trade, and while such laws were in some degree repugnant to strict constitutional principle, in practice they were of mutual benefit as long as their aim was the furtherance of commerce.

Since they have been distorted into revenue measures, however, the situation has materially changed: "Taxation and representation are in their nature inseparable; the right of withholding or of giving and granting of their own money, is the only effective security to a free people against the encroachments of despotism and tyranny." Furthermore, in attempting to raise revenue, Parliament is presuming that the colonies fail to recognize their duty to contribute in proportion to their circumstances to the defense of the Empire of which they are a part. Such a presumption is false, and during the late war was proved to be so.

The cause of Boston is the common cause of all British America; if the destruction of tea in Boston harbor be regarded as an infringement of private property, the signers of these resolves are willing to contribute toward paying for it, but no subsequent purchases from the East India Company should be made until grievances are redressed: Nothing will be of more value in obtaining redress than a firm union:

A Congress should be appointed, to consist of deputies from all the colonies, to concert a general and uniform plan for the defence and preservation of our common rights, and continuing the connexion and dependence of the said

[33]

colonies upon Great Britain under a just, lenient, permanent, and constitutional form of government.

Thanks are tendered to the friends of liberty in Great Britain who are exerting themselves in the interest of constitutional right.

A solemn covenant or association should be entered into by the several colonies covering a series of economic measures: domestic manufactures should be stimulated by premiums; only a very strictly limited list of articles should be imported, and after a year even they should be discontinued; in particular, no slaves should be received—"We take this opportunity of declaring our most earnest wishes to see an entire stop forever put to such a wicked, cruel and unnatural trade." If redress be not obtained by November 1, 1775, no exports should be shipped to Great Britain from any of the colonies. Relations should be broken off with any colony failing to accede to the association.

If Boston be forced to submit, Congress should agree upon measures to preserve the lives, liberties, and fortunes of the rest. Meanwhile the deputies in Congress should

draw up & transmit an humble & dutiful petition & remonstrance to his Majesty, asserting with decent firmness our just & constitutional rights & privileges . . . declaring, in the strongest terms, our duty & affection . . . beseeching his Majesty not to reduce his faithful subjects of America to a state of desperation, & to reflect, that from our sovereign there can be but one appeal.

These Resolves were transmitted to the convention in August. Every sort of advice was in the air. Thomson Mason had been publishing a series of letters, signed "A British American," in which he advised the colonies to recognize no parliamentary laws since 4 James I, the date of the first settlement in Virginia, as binding upon them. The Albemarle Resolutions, written by Jefferson, put forth the view that Parliament could not rightly legislate for the colonies in any case whatsoever. Jefferson's ideas, subsequently printed in "A Summary View of the Rights of British America," along with those in James Wilson's "Considerations," were strongly in men's minds. Both in the Convention and in the Continental Congress at Philadelphia, however, the more moderate view contained in the Fairfax Resolves was accepted as representative of public opinion.

Meanwhile, there was more activity in the counties. Toward the end of September, Mason presided at a session in Fairfax which adopted his plan for the creation of the Fairfax Independent Company of volunteers. Its purpose was somewhat thinly veiled by a reference to the Indians; the specifications as to dress and equipment included, besides "a regular uniform of blue, turned up with buff, with plain yellow metal buttons, buff waistcoat and breeches & white stockings . . . a good flint lock & bayonet, sling cartouche box *and tomahawk.*" (It was Washington's affection for the uniform of this, his first American command, that made him continue to use it himself and prescribe it for his personal guard when he became commander-in-chief.)

In June, 1775, in proposing annual elections of the company's officers, to institute rotation in office, Mason said:

We came equals into this world, and equals we shall go out of it. All men are by nature born equally free and independent. To protect the weaker from the injuries and insults of the stronger were societies first formed: when men entered into compacts to give up some of their natural rights, that by union and mutual assistance they might secure the rest; but they gave up no more that the nature of the thing required. Every society, all government, and every kind of civil compact therefore, is or ought to be, calculated for the general good and safety of the community . . . whenever any power or authority whatever extends further, or is of longer duration than is in its nature necessary for these purposes, it may be called government, but it is in fact oppression. . . . To prevent these fatal effects . . . the most effectual means . . . is frequently appealing to the body of the people . . . for their approbation or dissent. . . . In all our associations, in all our agreements, let us never lose sight of this fundamental maxim—that all power was originally lodged in, and consequently is derived from, the people.

Bulwarked by these political precepts, a motion in favor of rotation was carried, only to be immediately subjected to an exception "in favor of the gentleman who by the unanimous voice of the company now commands it" (Washington), which exception, Mason declared, "is a very proper one, justly due to his public merit & experience; it is peculiarly suited to our circumstances, & was dictated, not by compliment, but by conviction."

During the spring of 1775 military organization had become general. At the second Virginia convention, the end of March, Patrick Henry brought in a motion for a colony-wide militia, supported it by his speech containing the slogan, "Give me liberty or give me death," and, to the satisfaction of the Movement Party, got it passed.

If to some his action had seemed hasty, two events in the succeeding month changed their point of view. On April 20, Governor Dunmore ordered the removal of the powder in the Williamsburg magazine to British warships in the river; on April 19 a similar British attempt to take over military stores in New England led to the battles of Lexington and Concord.

News of the battles galloped rapidly southward; on the 27th it reached Patrick Henry. He called a meeting in Hanover County to reconsider the affair of the Williamsburg powder, and started to move on the city, sending ahead a messenger to the king's revenue collector demanding payment for the transferred stores. The Governor took alarm, sent his family aboard a warship and said that if any injury was offered to himself or the officers who acted under his directions, he would proclaim liberty to the slaves and reduce Williamsburg to ashes. The new opposition paper, *Purdie's Gazette,* proclaimed "The sword is now drawn, & God knows when it will be sheathed," but after the receiver-general issued a bond for £320 (twice the value of the powder) Henry retired.

When the Governor convened the Assembly June 1 to hear Lord North's "Olive Branch" resolution, the Speaker of the Burgesses, Peyton Randolph, was freshly returned from presiding over the Second Continental Congress. Two nights later, some young bloods of Williamsburg attempted to enter the powder magazine and were badly injured by a spring gun which Dunmore had ordered trained on the entrance. On the 8th, the Governor fled to a warship. The Burgesses continued to transact business without him, framing a reply to Lord North, passing bills to cover the cost of the war with the Indians.

It was their last session under royal government. In the autumn, Dunmore declared martial law. He spent the succeeding months attacking the coastal counties from the water, burning Norfolk in January 1776 and carrying on sporadic raids until his return to England at the end of the year.

Meanwhile, the colonies were arming on a continental basis. On June 15, 1775 the Continental Congress appointed George Washington commander-in-chief of the combined colonial forces; a few weeks later it issued a "Declaration of the Causes and Necessity of Taking up Arms"; Washington proceeded to Boston; military operations began.

The third Virginia convention met at Richmond July 17. A week after its opening, Mason, whom the insistence of his neighbors had finally forced into office, wrote Martin Cockburn:

The committee (of which I am a member) appointed to prepare an ordinance for raising an armed force for the defence and protection of this colony, meet every morning at seven o'clock, sit till the Convention meets, which seldom rises before five in the afternoon, and immediately after dinner and a little refreshment sits again till nine or ten at night. This is hard duty, and yet we have hitherto made but little progress, and I think shall not be able to bring in the ordinance till late next week, if then. This will not be wondered at when the extent and importance of the business before us is reflected on.

The scheme for consolidating Virginia's military forces was complete by the middle of August, and Patrick Henry chosen commander-in-chief. On the 17th a Committee of Safety consisting of seventeen members was elected to serve the colony as an executive; and Mason's attempt to decline membership was met with a determined refusal.

His general impression of the Convention is expressed in a letter to Washington, written in October after he was back at Gunston Hall:

I wrote to you in July, a little before my being ordered to the Convention, congratulating you upon an appointment which gives so much satisfaction to all America. . .

During the first part of the Convention, parties ran so high, that we had frequently no other way of preventing improper measures but by procrastination, urging the previous question, and giving men time to reflect. However, after some weeks, the babblers were pretty well silenced, a few weighty members began to take the lead, several wholesome regulations were made, and, if the Convention had continued to sit for a few days longer, I think the public safety would have been as well provided for as our present circumstances permit.

Mason spent the next seven months, as his letters to Washington and the Journal of the Committee of Safety show, in carrying out the details of military preparation on the Potomac. He was reelected as a delegate to the December convention, but prevented from attending by a fit of the gout; for this reason he also asked that his name be dropped from the Committee of Safety.

The first months of 1776 saw a definite crystallization of political attitude. The publication, on January 10, of Thomas Paine's pamphlet, "Common Sense," had perhaps as much to do with this change as any single piece of argumentative writing. It was avidly read. When the May convention met, copies of John Adams' "Thoughts on Government" were ready for distribution.

The instructions which the county meetings gave to their delegates were vivid: Cumberland, on April 22, announced that "we, therefore, your constituents, instruct you positively to declare for an independency, that you solemnly abjure any Allegeance to his Brittanick majesty & bid him a good night forever." Charlotte, one day later, urged its representative to "use your best endeavours that the Delegates which are sent to the General Congress be instructed immediately to cast off the British yoke."

On May 15 the convention unanimously announced:

Wherefore, appealing to the Searcher of Hearts for the Sincerity of former declarations expressing our desire to preserve the connection with that nation, and that we are driven from that inclination by their wicked councils, and the eternal law of self-preservation:

Resolved unanimously, that the Delegates appointed to represent this Colony in General Congress be instructed to propose to that respectable body to declare the United Colonies free & independent states . . .

Resolved, unanimously, that a committee be appointed to prepare a DECLARA-
TION OF RIGHTS & such a plan of Government as will be most likely to maintain peace & order in this Colony, & secure substantial & equal liberty to the
people.

X

THE DECLARATION OF RIGHTS
AND THE CONSTITUTION OF VIRGINIA

On the day after the passage of the instruction for independence, the
Virginia convention held but the briefest of sessions; celebrations were
in order. In reporting the toasts drunk to the American independent
states, to the Congress and the state legislatures, and to General Washington and victory to the American arms, while the Union flag waved
above the Capitol, *Purdie's Gazette* dropped from its masthead the royal
coat of arms and motto, *En dat Virginia quartam,* and substituted:

THIRTEEN UNITED COLONIES
"United we stand—Divided, we fall".

But if the 16th was given over to unrestrained rejoicing, the day after
found the legislators in a compensatingly sober mood. By coincidence
it was the day appointed by the Continental Congress as a General
Fast; in the hush of this somber afternoon, Mason arrived at the capital.
He was immediately added to the committee which had been appointed
three days before to prepare a declaration of rights and constitution.

Dubious of the value of some of his colleagues, he sat down that very
day to write to Richard Henry Lee urging him to come back from Congress to participate in the forthcoming deliberations:

After a smart fit of the gout, which detained me at home the first of the
session, I have at last reached this place, where, to my great satisfaction, I find
the first grand point has been carried *nem. con.,* the opponents being so few
that they did not think fit to divide or contradict the general voice. Your brother,
Col. T., will enclose you the resolve. The preamble is tedious, rather timid, and
in many cases exceptionable, but I hope it may answer the purpose. We are now
going upon the most important of all subjects—government! The committee
appointed to prepare a plan is, according to custom, overcharged with useless
members. You know our Convention. I need not say that it is not mended by
the recent elections. We shall, in all probability, have a thousand ridiculous and
impracticable proposals, and of course a plan formed of heterogeneous, jarring
and unintelligible ingredients. This can be prevented only by a few men of
integrity and abilities, whose country's interest lies next their hearts, under-
taking this business and defending it ably through every stage of opposition.

I need not tell you how much you will be wanted here on this occasion. I speak with the sincerity of a friend, when I assure you that, in my opinion, your presence cannot, must not, be dispensed with.

In a little over a week the committee reported out a draft Declaration of Rights; it was discussed in detail; on June 12 it was unanimously adopted. In spite of the prolonged discussion, the original draft presented by Mason was to an amazing extent retained in its entirety. Preservation in the State Library at Richmond of a copy of the original, which Mason sent to George Mercer in 1778, makes possible a comparison between the document as he drafted it and the one finally adopted.

Virginia Declaration of Rights in 1776, Copy of First D(r)aught by G. M.

A Declaration of Rights made by the Representatives of the good people of Virginia, assembled in full and free convention, which rights do pertain to them and their posterity as the basis and foundation of government.

1. That all men are created equally free and independent, and have certain inherent natural rights, of which they cannot, by any compact, deprive or divest their posterity; among which are the enjoyment of life and liberty, with the means of acquiring and possessing property, and pursuing and obtaining happiness and safety.

2. That all power is by God and Nature vested in, and consequently derived from, the people; that magistrates are their trustees and servants, and at all times amenable to them.

3. That government is, or ought to be, instituted for the common benefit, protection, and security of the people, nation, or community. Of all the various modes and forms of government, that is best which is capable of producing the greatest degree of happiness and safety, and is most effectively secured against the dangers of mal-administration; and that whenever any government shall be found inadequate or contrary to these purposes, a majority of the community hath an indubitable, unalienable, and indefeasible right to reform, alter or abolish it, in such a manner as shall be judged most conducive to the public weal.

4. That no man, or set of men, are entitled to exclusive or separate emoluments or privileges from the community, but in consideration of public services; which not being descendible, neither ought the offices of magistrate, legislator, or judge to be hereditary.

5. That the legislative and executive powers of the State should be separate and distinct from the judicial; and that the members of the two first may be restrained from oppression by feeling and participating the burthens of the people, they should, at fixed periods, be reduced to a private station, and return to that body from which they were originally taken, and the vacancies be supplied by frequent, certain, and regular elections.

6. That elections of members to serve as representatives of the people in the legislature ought to be free, and that all men, having sufficient evidence of

permanent, common interest with and attachment to the community, have the right of suffrage, and cannot be taxed, or deprived of their property for public uses, without their own consent, or that of their representatives, so elected, nor bound by any law to which they have not, in like manner, assented for the common good.

7. That all power of suspending laws, or the execution of laws, by any authority, without consent of the representatives of the people, is injurious to their rights, and ought not to be exercised.

8. That in all capital or criminal prosecutions, a man hath a right to demand the cause and nature of his accusation, to be confronted with the accusers and witnesses, to call for evidence in his favor, and to a speedy trial by an impartial jury of his vicinage, without whose unanimous consent he cannot be found guilty, nor can he be compelled to give evidence against himself; and that no man be deprived of his liberty, except by the law of the land or the judgment of his peers.

9. That excessive bail ought not to be required, nor excessive fines imposed, nor cruel and unusual punishments inflicted.

10. That in controversies respecting property, and in suits between man and man, the ancient trial by jury is preferable to any other, and to be held sacred.

11. That the freedom of the press is one of the great bulwarks of liberty, and can never be restrained but by despotic governments.

12. That a well regulated militia, composed of the body of the people, trained to arms, is the proper, natural and safe defence of a free state; that standing armies in time of peace should be avoided, as dangerous to liberty; and that in all cases, the military should be under strict subordination to, and governed by, the civil power.

13. That no free government, or the blessing of liberty, can be preserved to any people but by a firm adherence to justice, moderation, temperance, frugality and virtue, and by frequent recurrence to fundamental principles.

14. That religion, or the duty which we owe our Creator and the manner of discharging it, can be directed only by reason and conviction, not by force or violence; and, therefore, that all men should enjoy the fullest toleration in the exercise of religion, according to the dictates of conscience, unpunished and unrestrained by the magistrate, unless, under color of religion, any man disturb the peace, the happiness, or the safety of society. And that it is the mutual duty of all to practise Christian forbearance, love, and charity towards each other.

As a footnote to this copy, Mason wrote, "This Declaration of Rights was the first in America; it received few alterations or additions in the Virginia Convention (some of them not for the better) and was afterwards closely imitated by the other United States." The alterations, in all but a few cases, were largely textual. The additions consisted of two articles, of which the first, in uneasy memory of British practice, declared against the issuance of general warrants; the second affirmed that no government separate from the government of Virginia should be established within her territorial limits.

The development of Mason's ideas can for the most part be definitely traced through his previous writings; their wording in many instances literally repeats the phrases of his county papers. The first five sections and the thirteenth grew naturally out of his address to the Fairfax Independent Company; the next five are derived from the catalogue of British abuses which he drew up as part of the Fairfax Resolves; the twelfth is condensed from the Proceedings of the Fairfax County Committee of January 17, 1775. The two sections whose subject matter he had not previously treated were the eleventh, on freedom of the press, and the fourteenth, on religious toleration, but he had had background in these areas through the succession of Williamsburg newspapers and the clash in Truro Parish between establishment and dissent.

The Declaration differed in an important respect from the great English documents that preceded it, from Magna Charta to the Bill of Rights of 1689. These lists of grievances, like the petitions and remonstrances of the American colonial assemblies, were addressed to a known sovereign. In the case of Mason's Declaration, as in the case of the French *déclaration des droits de l'homme* which followed after it, the form of the future government was as yet undetermined; consequently, the enumerated rights served as a positive "basis and foundation of government."

The theory of the nature of civil society stated in Mason's first sections parallels, almost point for point, that of Locke's second "Treatise of Civil Government." The leading Virginia constitutionalists all made a point that individuals who form a society reserve to themselves certain powers; the subsequent extension of this concept to the rights of the individual state upon entering a union of states made it of cardinal importance not only in 1787-88, but again in 1861. In similar accord with Locke, all power is declared to be vested in the people. The magistrates are their trustees; government exists to further their happiness and safety; and should it fail to achieve that end, a right to resume the exercise of their powers is vested in a majority of the people. The consent principle is to be rigorously maintained in respect to taxation. Except in recognition of public service none shall have a privileged position in, or emoluments from, the community, and no honors are to be hereditary. The right to be voted for is declared to be general; the right to vote is conditioned by a man's having "sufficient evidence of permanent common interest with and attachment to the community." Freedom is to be safeguarded by a free press and by maintenance of the military in subordination to the civil power, but its abuse is to be watched.

At one point both Mason and Jefferson modified Locke's trinity of natural rights—"life, liberty, and property." They distinguished between property itself and opportunity to obtain it. Mason, in writing the Declaration of Rights, substituted "the means of acquiring and possessing property and pursuing and obtaining happiness and safety." Jefferson, in putting only "the pursuit of happiness" into the Declaration of Independence, carried the change still further.

The position and powers of the judiciary were regarded as crucial: four out of Mason's fourteen articles are devoted to legal safeguards; when the Federal Constitution was considered in Virginia in 1788, the most prolonged of all the discussions centered on the judiciary article.

After passage of the Declaration of Rights, the next task was to establish governmental agencies through which the principles of the Declaration could be expressed. The constitution which the convention adopted was among the first written constitutions for the governance of civil society. It was the first of the Revolutionary documents to be drawn after passage of a resolution for independence and hence designed as a permanent basis for an independent state—it endured without change well into the nineteenth century.

While the constitution was substantially Mason's work, the absence of a first draft in his handwriting makes impossible exact comparison between his plan and the form finally adopted. A number of able alternatives written by Virginians of various leanings, were in the field. Adams' "Thoughts on Government" had been widely circulated in Virginia. Jefferson, who was attending Congress at the time, sent down a draft, but it arrived the day the committee version reached the convention floor. Its preamble, however, which anticipated the main body of the Declaration of Independence, was adopted as a prefix.

The constitution, as unanimously approved on June 29, opened with a declaration that the powers of the legislative, executive, and judiciary departments should be separate. The legislature, or General Assembly, was to meet annually, and consist of two branches, a House of Delegates made up of two representatives from each county and one from each of certain cities, and a Senate of twenty-four members chosen from as many newly created districts. Members of both houses were to be freeholders or otherwise duly qualified and resident in the area they represented. The right to suffrage was unaltered from the colonial system. All legislation was to originate in the House; the powers of the Senate were confined to the veto and the amending power; and in the case of money bills to outright acceptance or rejection, with no power of amendment.

A governor was to be chosen annually by joint ballot of both Houses; he should not serve for more than three years in any seven. He should exercise the executive powers with the advice of a Council of State, and "alone have the direction of the militia under the laws of the country." For maladministration or corruption he was to be subject to impeachment by the House. The privy council to act with him, whose president was to be lieutenant governor, should consist of eight members, elected by joint ballot of both houses. The treasurer, an annual contingent of delegates to the Continental Congress, the judges of the high courts, the secretary, and the attorney-general were to be similarly elected and together with all others holding lucrative offices, and ministers of the gospel, should be ineligible to seats in the Assembly or the Council. All fines, escheats, etc., formerly going to the king, should go to the Commonwealth, in whose name and over whose seal all commissions and grants should run.

Protests against certain sections of the constitution were almost immediately made; some of them were sufficiently well-founded to lead to its amendment in the course of the nineteenth century. The division of power between governor and legislature paralyzed the governor while leaving the legislature's exuberance unrestrained. Little satisfaction was felt with the operation of the privy council; Madison pronounced it "a grave of useful talents." The most important objections, however, were to certain portions of the constitution which had been taken over from the colonial system—the county basis for representation, and the property qualifications for suffrage.

The qualifications of the right to vote and the proportioning of representatives to electors were crucial considerations in the developing sectional struggle in the legislature between the propertied aristocracy that paid most of the taxes and the rising upland democracy that furnished most of the militia. The constitution of 1776 institutionalized the aristocratic *status quo*. Five years after its adoption, Jefferson, in his "Notes on Virginia," pointed out that the roll of freeholders generally included less than one half the names on the roll of the militia or the list of the tax collectors, and that geographic disproportion was even greater. The inhabitants of Tidewater, close to the seat of government, lacked only four members of a majority of the House and controlled the destinies of the far greater number of Virginians living to the westward.

In 1783, Jefferson and Madison exchanged considerable correspondence on the possibility of a revisory convention. Regarding Mason's attitude, Jefferson wrote Madison: "You have seen G. M. I hope and had much conversation with him. What are his sentiments as to the amendment of our Constitution? What amendments would he oppose? Is he determined to sleep on, or will he rouse and be active? I wish to hear from you on this subject." The letter crossed one from Madison saying, "On the article of the Convention for revising our form of state government he was sound and ripe and I think would not decline a participation in the work." But Jefferson shortly departed for France and the movement to call a convention subsided.

At the beginning of July, 1776, however, the task before the convention was not to discover the weaknesses but to implement the strengths of the document it had just completed. In the election of a governor and council, the conservatives nominated Thomas Nelson, Sr., for the executive office; the Movement Party, Patrick Henry; Henry won by a vote of 65-45. Mason was chairman of the committee which notified him of his election, and installed him in the Governor's Palace from which, just over a year before, Lord Dunmore had issued a proclamation urging that "the said Patrick Henry" receive no aid from anyone. Mason was also chairman of the committee that designed the great seal of the Commonwealth, depicting on the one side, Libertas, Ceres, and Aeternitas, and on the other, above the motto SIC SEMPER TYRANNIS, "Virtus . . . dressed like an Amazon . . . treading on Tyranny." With constitutional independence thus established, the last of the Virginia conventions adjourned.

XI

THE COMMONWEALTH OF VIRGINIA

The first Assembly under the new constitution gathered in the autumn of 1776 to commence translation of the abstract principles of the Declaration of Rights into specific measures. The vigor with which the members of the Movement Party began their task is plain from Jefferson's note in his Autobiography:

> I had many occasional and strenuous coadjutors in debate, and one most steadfast, able and zealous, who was himself a host. This was George Mason, a man of the first order of wisdom among those who acted on the theatre of the Revolution, of expansive mind, profound judgment, cogent in argument, learned in the lore of our former constitution, and earnest for the republican change on democratic principles. His elocution was neither flowing nor smooth, but his language was strong, his manner most impressive, and strengthened by a dash of biting cynicism when provocation made it seasonable.

[44]

Mason served as a Fairfax County delegate in the assembly until the end of 1780. The first principal project with which he was associated was a general clarification of the law. Full powers were entrusted to a committee of five "Revisors," Jefferson, Pendleton, Wythe, Mason and T. L. Lee.

At their first meeting, Pendleton and Lee favored codification, on the model of Roman law, while Jefferson, Mason and Wythe preferred retention of the English common-law, with alterations only. Mason's notes run:

> The common law not to be meddled with, except where alterations are necessary. The statutes to be revised and digested, alterations proper for us to be made; the diction where obsolete or redundant, to be reformed; but otherwise to undergo as few changes as possible. The acts of the English Commonwealth to be examined. The statutes to be divided into periods; the acts of Assembly made on the same subject to be incorporated into them. The laws of the other colonies to be examined, and any good ones to be adopted.

Mason's assignment included the criminal law and the land law, but since he was a constitutionalist rather than a lawyer, he expressed doubts about his fitness for the detailed examination of individual statutes. After the broad outlines of the work were sketched, he resigned, though he subsequently drew bills for establishing a land office and settling land grant claims; the Committee was also diminished by the death of T. L. Lee.

The 126 bills which the remaining Revisors presented in 1779 offered a framework for a new and very different society; included were measures to abolish primogeniture, limit slavery, provide general education, and establish religious liberty. Some of these proposals were far ahead of anything the Assembly had currently in mind, but others fitted its mood: it had already abolished entail, and in exempting dissenters from payment of tithes it had taken a first step in revising the position of the established church.

The concern for the free exercise of religion displayed in the Declaration of Rights fitted not only the prevailing religious conviction but the rising desire for social equality. Among Virginia institutions, the Church of England had very graphically exhibited the eighteenth-century pattern of privilege. Its clergy were ordained overseas by the Bishop of London and confirmed in their appointment by the royal governor; their tenure was assured; their support bulked large in local taxation. Local privilege, moreover, was highly visible at church services; court-enforced attendance insured the presence of the entire community, and church seating reflected the gradations of social position.

How this society looked from a back pew can be gathered from the autobiography of Devereux Jarratt, who became an Anglican minister but started life as an orphan apprenticed to a carpenter:

We were accustomed to look upon gentle folks as beings of a superior order. For my part I was quite shy of them, and kept off at a humble distance. A periwig in those days was a distinguishing badge of gentlefolk, and when I saw a man riding the road, near our house with a wig on, it would so alarm my fears and give me such a disagreeable feeling, that I dare say I would run off as for my life.

The initial contest occurred in the committee charged with the preparation of the Declaration of Rights; the adoption of the unequivocal statement of the liberal position contained in Mason's fourteenth article was a decided victory for the advanced group of churchmen. So also was the act, framed by a committee of which Mason was chairman and passed at the first session of the Assembly under the constitution, exempting "the different societies of Dissenters from contributing to the support and maintenance of the church as by law established." It repealed all acts of Parliament directed against the sects, and relieved them of all levies except for the poor; at the same time it secured to the Church of England its real property, endowments, plate. This measure deprived the Church of England of its unique position but did not settle the general question of establishment; repeal, in 1779, of the former act authorizing church levies likewise left undetermined the attitude to be adopted by the Commonwealth. The first positive proposal was presented when the Committee of Law Revisors' Statute of Religious Freedom declared: "No man shall be compelled to frequent or support any religious worship, place or ministry whatsoever, but all men shall be free to profess, and by argument to maintain their opinion in matters of religion."

Legislative opinion was too much divided for this measure to pass immediately; while it lay tabled, the alternative desired by the conservatives began to gain ground. In 1784 they introduced their bill to include in the general state taxes a tithe for the support of religion; it was on the verge of passing when Madison succeeded in getting the vote postponed until the next session. During the recess, widespread circulation was given to a "Remonstrance" against the assessment, written by Madison at the suggestion of Mason and George Nicholas. When the Assembly reconvened, the Statute of Religious Freedom as drafted by Jefferson was carried. At the same time an Act of Incorporation transformed the former Church of England into the Protestant Episcopal Church, and organized the Diocese of Virginia.

But the practice of republican institutions was altering the composition of the legislature: In 1786 the new majority repealed the Act of Incorporation, and two years later, all laws relating to the "late Protestant

Episcopal Church." In the years that followed, their property confiscated, many of the Church of England churches in Truro and other Virginia parishes fell into a ruin that was close to complete.

At the same time that domestic issues such as law reform and church reorganization were claiming the attention of the legislators, increasingly insistent demands were coming from the frontier regarding the boundaries of the commonwealth. Settlers of Virginia origin along the Ohio River were anxious to know what government would furnish them protection. The inhabitants of the Kentucky country, in June, 1776, voted for adherence to Virginia, and sent John Gabriel Jones and George Rogers Clark to represent them before the Convention; at the next session, Kentucky was organized as a county of Virginia.

Clark went back, but a larger idea kept simmering in his mind. In the course of several visits to the eastern part of the state, he had come greatly under Mason's influence; and the concept contained in Mason's "Extracts from the Virginia Charters" had caught his imagination. In the autumn of 1777 he returned to Williamsburg with a bold proposal under his coonskin cap. Henry, Wythe, Mason, and Jefferson thought very well indeed of it; when Clark departed he had in his pocket authorization to take Kaskaskia from the British, and proceeded to conquer the area from Louisville to Detroit.

Clark's conquest of the Northwest Territory settled the question of sovereignty between the British and the Americans, but three different types of internal disputes about the lands it included remained to be settled.

In the realm of private rights, there were the conflicting claims of a mushroom growth of development companies which sprang into being overnight. Mason worked untiringly to see that an efficient land office was provided at Williamsburg.

Two conflicts of public jurisdiction remained to be settled. One concerned the western portions of the boundary lines between Virginia and North Carolina and Virginia and Pennsylvania, left vague during the period when settlement was largely confined to lands east of the mountains; in order to further the interstate comity on which the American Confederation depended, Mason urged Virginia to sacrifice claims regarding these lines whose legal status he considered wholly defensible.

And he maintained this same attitude on a still larger scale when the western lands question became a thorn in the side of the Confederation.

Four states—Connecticut, Massachusetts, New York, and Virginia—had claims to large tracts beyond the mountains. The smaller states, seeing the danger to the balance of power, insisted that title to the undeveloped territories should be transferred to the Confederation.

When the matter was taken up in the Continental Congress, Joseph Jones, one of the Virginia delegates, asked Mason to prepare a draft for a settlement; his reply advocated that all territory north of the Ohio, after safeguards had been taken to fulfill Virginia's commitments to her soldiers, be ceded to the United States.

This paper was Mason's final contribution to the destiny of the Northwest Territory. Following cessions by the other interested states, the American Congress, under Jefferson's leadership, framed the Northwest Ordinance and provided for the creation and admission to the Union of Indiana, Ohio, Illinois, Michigan, Wisconsin, and part of Minnesota.

But while Clark's campaigns were succeeding along the Mississippi, the Revolution proper was making only dubious progress along the eastern coast. The Continental Congress was actually a congress of ambassadors; the jealous particularism of the individual states left it without resources of its own, and though it attempted to remedy its deficiencies by assuming ungranted powers, it was impotent to carry its resolutions and requisitions, of money or of men, beyond the declaratory stage.

The inefficiency and personal chicanery contingent upon this inadequate governmental framework made the most able men in the community progressively less willing to participate in public life. Washington's letter to Mason of March 27, 1779, shows the despair of the man whose position enabled him to assess the overall situation better than any other:

I have seen without despondency (even for a moment) the hours which America has styled her gloomy ones—but I have beheld no day since the commencement of hostilities, that I have thought her liberties in such imminent danger as at the present. Friends and foes seem now to combine to pull down the goodly fabric we have hitherto been raising at the expense of so much time, blood, and treasure, and unless the bodies politic will exert themselves to bring things back to first principles, correct abuses, and punish our internal foes, inevitable ruin must follow. Indeed we seem to be verging so fast upon destruction, that I am filled with sensations to which I have been a stranger till within these three months. Our enemy behold with exultation and joy, how effectively we labor for their benefit, and from being in a state of absolute despair and on the point of evacuating America, are now on tiptoe. Nothing, therefore, in my judgment, can save us but a total reformation in our conduct, or some decisive turn to affairs in Europe. . . .

Where are our men of abilities? Let this voice, my dear sir, call upon you, Jefferson, and others. Do not—from a mistaken opinion that we are about to sit down under our own vine and our own fig tree—let our hitherto noble struggle end in ignominy. Believe me when I tell you there is danger of it.

Mason's letter to Richard Henry Lee, who in May resigned from the

Continental Congress in disgust, verified that the best men were increasingly staying at home:

> I had almost forgot to inform you of our new election of members to Congress; it is indeed a disagreeable subject . . . and I think you will hardly blame me for taking care in time to keep out of such company.

In 1780 Mason decided to keep out of even the company that the Assembly afforded, and retired to Gunston. But as the theater for the final act of the war shifted to Virginia, British raids in the rivers and the northward advance from Charleston of the main body of enemy troops made the military situation increasingly real.

The year before, Jefferson had succeeded Henry as governor; he came increasingly under attack as British incursions increased and citizens began to search for a scapegoat; Mason and he were in more or less continuous correspondence.

In the spring of 1781, Mason wrote to the Virginia delegation in Congress, expressing doubts as to the success of the American cause unless a strong French fleet could be brought into cooperation with the American land forces. He urged that a vigorous representation of the facts be made in Paris, and a few weeks later expressed the same sentiments in a letter to his son George, which Franklin showed to the Duc de Vergennes and which was quite possibly of influence in the transfer of the French command in America from D'Estaing to De Grasse.

The battle of Yorktown and the end of the war in America removed the physical danger, but made only a negative difference in the disintegration into which public life was falling. Jefferson's horseback accident and Mason's increasingly serious attacks of "convulsive colic" were no more than ostensible reasons for retirement from a political situation that disgusted them. Practically every one of Mason's public letters at this time contains some such paragraph as that written to Edmund Randolph in October 1782:

> I quitted my seat in the House of Delegates, from a conviction that I was no longer able to do any essential service. Some of the public measures have been so contrary to my notions of policy and of justice that I wished to be no further concerned with, or answerable for them; and to spend the remnant of my life in quiet and retirement. Yet with all her faults, my country will ever have my warmest wishes and affections; and I would at any time, most cheerfully sacrifice my own ease and domestic enjoyments to the public good.

Two years later Mason again refused to allow a poll to be opened in his name for the Assembly, but in 1786 he abandoned his retirement because of his interest in two issues.

The first was financial. The close of hostilities had not ended the chaos of the currency. A crisis accumulated, in which most states turned again to their printing presses for relief. Virginia was one of the few states which resisted temptation, and Mason, in a letter to Jefferson in France, indicates that her abstention was due to his efforts.

The other issue which attracted Mason once more into public affairs, and led him to serve for the first time outside the boundaries of his own state, was the new-modeling of the continental frame of government.

Few could be found to deny that the Articles of Confederation were inadequate, and the choice between chaos and reconstruction was becoming daily clearer. In 1783, military dictatorship was just around the corner. In 1778, in order to keep the army together, Congress had promised the officers a bonus of half pay for life; for the succeeding five years it had produced no pay at all. As one of the Confederation's most important creditors, the army was reluctant to disband before collecting; Washington headed off a coup d'etat, but his veterans remained a bulwark of sentiment in favor of a strong central government with inherent powers.

The interests of trade pointed in the same direction as the interests of the army. Except in the most limited of local areas, the exchange of goods was rendered almost impossible by financial instability, by tariff warfare in which each of the states was seeking its own advantage, and by the absence of general commercial treaties with foreign nations.

The Confederation was not only falling off in popular regard; it was very nearly ceasing to exist. The Congressional session of 1784 was a failure; four states did not send representatives, and the spokesmen of three others became disgusted and withdrew, leaving no alternative to adjournment for lack of a quorum.

As early as 1780 plans for a new constitution had begun to make their appearance; from time to time Congress itself appointed committees to suggest amendments to the Articles of Confederation, and new projects were continually circulating in private letters. In 1787 the work of reorganization was undertaken.

By a curious irony, the first step towards the Convention that consummated it was the conclusion of a treaty between Virginia and Maryland, of whose existence the legislature of the Commonwealth of Virginia, though fully cognizant of the fact that the sixth of the Articles of Confederation declared it illegal for states to make treaties with each other without the consent of Congress, voted that that no longer very august body should not even be informed.

XII

THE FORMATION OF THE FEDERAL UNION

Faith in the Potomac River as a "channel of the extensive trade of a rising empire" was actively shared by many gentlemen in Maryland and Virginia, Mason and Washington included. But both the future development of the river and its existing status were a frequent cause of friction. At the end of 1784, the Virginia Assembly appointed four commissioners, Mason, Edmund Randolph, Madison, and Alexander Henderson, to meet with commissioners from Maryland to deal with both economic and political issues and appointed Washington to go to Annapolis to confer regarding bills for development companies; the Mount Vernon Convention was the result.

The convention itself regulated the minutiae of river life, but appended to it was a supplementary report covering very inclusive questions of defense, finance, and tariffs. Clearly, in these matters the two negotiating states were not the only ones whose interests were involved: Madison wrote Washington that a commercial league to include the whole union "seems naturally to grow out of the proposed appointment of Com^{srs} for Virg^a & Mary^d concerted at Mount Vernon," and persuaded the Virginia Assembly to call upon the members of the Confederation to send delegates to Annapolis "to take into consideration the trade of the United States."

Only five states were represented at Annapolis in September, 1786, and since the number was regarded as insufficient for the purpose which had brought them together, the meeting adjourned after four days. But before adjourning, its members issued a report written by Hamilton of New York with the assistance of Madison and Randolph of Virginia, recommending re-convention in Philadelphia the following May for a general reconstruction of the central government.

Virginia was the first state to approve the report and select as her commissioners to the Constitutional Convention, Washington, Henry (who declined to serve and was replaced by James McClurg), Edmund Randolph, John Blair, Madison, Mason, and Wythe.

It is clear that Mason, as he set out for Philadelphia, not only anticipated but approved a strengthening of the central government. It is equally clear that during the preceding years his views had undergone considerable change. Insistence on states' rights is the keynote of the "Address and Instructions of Their Constituents" delivered by the electors of Fairfax County to their delegates in the Assembly in 1783 and almost certainly drafted by Mason; Madison, who visited Gunston Hall in December, reported to Jefferson that Mason's private comments were also in this vein. But by the spring of 1781 Madison was reassured:

The prospect of a full and respectable convention grows stronger every day. . . . Our Governor, Mr. Wythe, Mr. Blair and Col. Mason will pretty certainly attend. The last, I am informed, is renouncing his errors on the subject of the Confederation, and means to take an active part in the amendment of it.

It is doubtless not a coincidence that Mason's recognition of the need for a central government followed resumption of neighbourly intercourse with Washington when the Commander-in-Chief returned to live once more at Mount Vernon, convinced by his war experience that "the honor, power and true Interest of this country must be measured by a Continental scale."

At any rate, Mason's first letter from Philadelphia to his son George includes:

The expectations and hopes of all the Union centre in this Convention. God grant that we may be able to concert effectual means of preserving our country from the evils which threaten us. . . . It is easy to foresee that there will be much difficulty in organizing a government upon this great scale, and at the same time reserving to the State legislatures a sufficient portion of power for promoting and securing the prosperity and happiness of their respective citizens; yet with a proper degree of coolness, liberality and candor (very rare commodities by the bye) I doubt not but it may be effected.

Since the Pennsylvania and Virginia delegations alone were complete at the time of his arrival on May 17, Mason and his colleagues had a week of preparatory leisure in their quarters at the "Indian Queen." For two or three hours daily they worked upon the proposal that became known as the "Virginia Plan."

On May 25, the number of states represented had reached seven, twenty-nine delegates were present, and the Convention got to work. Though sixty-five members had been appointed by the states, all but ten of whom took part in the sessions at one time or another, attendance was ordinarily not much higher that on the opening day. Most of the more conspicuous figures of the ensuing deliberations were then present: red-haired Alexander Hamilton, who was there for both the opening and the closing meetings, though the total time he spent in Philadelphia was relatively short; Gouverneur Morris, brilliant, erratic, excitedly punctuating his emphasis by thumps of his wooden leg; General Washington, with a calm in his eye sufficient to quell even the Morris temper; Madison, physically less striking but respected as a reservoir of political history. The stormy weather in which the Convention opened prevented the attendance of the eighty-one-year-old Benjamin Franklin, who was brought usually forward as a symbol of venerable detachment, whenever the situation required a ceremony or approached a crisis.

It had been intended that Franklin should open proceedings by nominating Washington for the presidency of the Convention; Robert Morris represented the Pennsylvania delegation in his stead. Unanimous approval of the choice, a short speech of acceptance, and the selection of a secretary and rules committee finished the first day's proceedings. On Tuesday, May 29 the real business at hand was taken up, with the presentation, by Governor Randolph, of the Virginia Plan. During the debates that followed, the five speakers who addressed the House most frequently were Sherman of Connecticut, James Wilson and Gouverneur Morris of Pennsylvania, and Madison and Mason of Virginia.

The decision to consider the Virginia Plan rather than to attempt a revision of the Articles of Confederation bore out an opinion which Mason had earlier hazarded in a letter to Arthur Lee:

> The most prevalent idea I think at present is a total change of the federal system, and instituting a great national council or parliament upon the principles of equal proportionate representation, consisting of two branches of the legislature invested with full legislative powers upon the objects of the Union; and to make the State legislatures subordinate to the national by giving the latter a negative upon all such laws as they judge contrary to the principles and interest of the Union; to establish also a national executive, and a judiciary system with cognizance of all such matters as depend upon the law of nations, and such other objects as the local courts of justice may be inadequate to.

When Mason said that the new legislature was to be based on "equal proportionate representation," he used in combination two adjectives which shortly became opposing slogans. The small states occupied the legally correct position that equality meant equal representation of the thirteen sovereigns on the principle of one state, one vote. The large states insisted that such a system would result not in equality but in minority rule; actual equality between a state like New Hampshire or New Jersey and a state like Massachusetts or Pennsylvania required proportionate recognition of differences in population and wealth.

The introduction of population and wealth as a possible basis for representation uncovered the Convention's second major divergence arising from sectional differences in economic interest. New England and the Middle States made their living by selling services, while the South made its living by selling commodities. So the planter was set off against the shipper and the trader, the producer against the middleman; and the difference was complicated by the fact that the South's production was based upon slavery.

In broadest terms, the task which the Convention had before it was to resolve two differences—one political and one economic; and to solve two problems—the constitutionally desirable form of federal executive and the source of federal authority.

The decision to use "We the people" rather than "We the States" as the source of constitutional power came fairly easily. No one knew how many States would accede to the new plan; furthermore, unless based directly on the people, the Constitution would be a treaty between states rather than the supreme law of the land. If it was to have independent validity, the fountain of its authority must be the same as that of the civil societies already organized; hence the phrase "We the States" was discarded and popular origin doubly safeguarded by providing that ratification of the document should be by specially-called popular conventions rather than by the state legislatures.

The decision as to the proper form of federal executive came hard: plan after plan was brought up, canvassed, and accepted or rejected only to reappear for reconsideration. The points of similarity between the proposed central government and the British crown were too obvious not to excite the emotions of '76 all over again. There were delegates, like Hamilton and Gouverneur Morris, who thought a strongly aristocratic rule, if not a kingship, the only enduring solution. There were delegates who saw in monarchy the root of all evil, whose convictions were democratic to the core, yet whose ten years' observation of the legislative follies of democracy, both in the Confederation and in the state governments, had convinced them of the necessity of a powerful executive. But should the executive be single or plural? how should he or they be chosen? for how long a term? how provided with advisers? by the Senate, by a cabinet of department heads, by the Supreme Court judges sitting as a revisionary council? how distinguished from the other departments of government? The final plan for selection was not brought in until September 4.

Throughout June, as the clauses of the Virginia Plan were considered, one after another had to be dropped because the question of representation in the legislature was too delicate to be touched. With each postponement, as Madison's careful record of the proceedings shows, the tension increased. By June 11 Franklin was brought in to warn:

Mr. Chairman . . . we are sent here to consult, not to contend, with each other; and declarations of fixed opinion and of determined resolution never to change it neither enlighten nor convince us.

The general temper did not improve as the days went by. By the end of the month even the possibility of partition of territory was being canvassed as a means of equalizing the power of the states.

Dissolution was in the air. Mason wrote Beverley Randolph:

Things . . . are now drawing to that point on which some of the fundamental principles must be decided, and two or three days will probably enable us to judge—which is at present very doubtful—whether any sound and effectual system can be established or not. If it cannot, I presume we shall not continue here much longer; if it can, we shall probably be detained 'til September.

On July 2, Pinckney of South Carolina proposed referring the problem to a committee of one member from each state, to be considered during the Independence Day recess.

If flies from an adjacent livery stable were helpful in 1776 in stinging the more reluctant delegates into signing the Declaration of Independence, the break which occurred in the damp summer heat of Philadelphia did as much to produce acceptance when the select committee—Mason was its Virginia member—reported the "Connecticut Compromise." The change in general feeling can be measured by the contrast between a few words from Mason's speech on July 5 and his discouraged letter of six days before. Madison records him as saying that

the Report was meant not as specific propositions to be adopted; but merely as a general ground of accomodation. There must be some accomodation at this point, or we shall make little further progress in the work. . . . It could not be more inconvenient to any gentleman to remain absent from his private affairs, than it was for him; but he would bury his bones in this City rather than expose his Country to the Consequences of a dissolution of the Convention without anything being done.

On July 16 the Compromise passed. The formula it provided for proportional representation in the lower house, based on the total free population plus three fifths of the slaves in each state, was not new; it was taken over bodily from the Confederation's revenue amendment of April 18, 1783. But its discussion had brought out new alignments, and with them, new antagonisms.

Sectionalism became so strong that some members saw no solution but the organization of two confederacies. The South wanted its exports to go out and its slaves to come in without governmental interference. The North wanted encouragement for its shipping and protection for its manufacturers. As soon as the Connecticut Compromise terminated the struggle over political representation, both sections moved to secure their economic interests.

By August 22 affairs had again reached a crisis, with the discussion running around a triangle whose three points were occupied respectively by Northern economic interests concentrated on the power to set tariffs by majority action, Southern economic interests concentrated on the power to hold slaves, and a third group, composed of both Northerners and Southerners, who wished to consider slavery as a social institution rather than as the raw materials of bargaining power.

As the leader of the third group, Mason made an impassioned speech denouncing continuation of the slave trade:

> This infernal traffic originated in the avarice of British merchants. The British government constantly checked the attempts of Virginia to put a stop to it. The present question concerns not the importing States alone but the whole Union. The evil of having slaves was experienced during the late war. Had slaves been treated as they might have been by the enemy, they would have proved dangerous instruments in their hands. . . . Slavery discourages arts and manufactures. The poor despise labor when performed by slaves. They prevent the immigration of whites who really enrich and strengthen a country. They produce the most pernicious effect on manners. Every master of slaves is born a petty tyrant. They bring the judgment of Heaven upon a country. As nations can not be rewarded or punished in the next world they must be in this.

South Carolina and Georgia repeated their ultimata, however, and Morris moved that the two clauses be referred to a committee: "these things may form a bargain among the Northern and Southern States." On August 25, New Hampshire, Massachusetts, Connecticut, Maryland, North Carolina, South Carolina, and Georgia outvoted New Jersey, Pennsylvania, Delaware, and Virginia to accept the bargain the committee had arranged.

The remaining two and a half weeks of the Convention were devoted to a clause-by-clause examination of the draft instrument. During this period of the work Mason spoke on almost every motion presented; a survey of his speeches, as preserved in Yate's jottings and in Madison's notes, indicates both the positive attitude which he had towards the Constitution up to a few days before its completion, and the extent to which his suggestions and the motions which he favored were and are incorporated in its various articles.

He was in favor of a bicameral legislature, meeting annually, in which the members of the lower house should be biennially elected on a suffrage basis determined by the respective states. They should be qualified as to citizenship and property, residents of the district they represent, and at least twenty-five years of age.

The number of representatives should be proportionate to the total number of freemen plus three fifths of the number of slaves in each state, and there should be periodical redistribution on the basis of a decennial census. Senators should be at least thirty years of age and subject to a property qualification. Their term of previous citizenship should be long, preferably fourteen years, so as to obviate the danger of a British lobby in matters of trade. While the lower house should be a large body in order to assemble broad information on the condition of the country, state interests could be adequately represented by two senators apiece. A majority should be required for a quorum, and the yeas and nays recorded on the desire of one fifth of the members present; an annual account of expenditures and of proceedings should be published, with the possible exception of such of the Senate debates as pertained to the treaty-making power. Members of both Houses should be paid by the United States, and as a safeguard against corruption they should be ineligible to offices created during their terms.

Mason's views on what was desirable for the executive coincided with the Constitution as adopted less closely than his views on the legislature. Like the rest of his colleagues, he changed his mind a number of times; his final conclusions seem to have been in favor of a plural executive of three persons, on the grounds that a single head is dangerous; when provision for a vice-president who should preside over the Senate was proposed, he objected to the office as an unsound mixture of the departments of government and as an encroachment on the rights of the Senate. But if a single executive were preferred, he should be elected for seven years—the principle of tenure of office during good behavior is suitable only for the judiciary—and not re-eligible, or perhaps not eligible for more than six in any twelve years. He should be removable by impeachment—not by the Senate, to which he is too closely related in various functions, but by the legislature. A two-thirds rather than a three-fourths vote should be sufficient to override his veto; his pardoning power should not include cases of treason, and his appointment power should be watched most carefully.

The executive should be advised by a council, of which the worst form would be a cabinet of department heads, a possible form a privy council of six, two from each section of the nation, and the most useful form a council of revision, made up of the Supreme Court judges who could exercise a general surveillance of the laws. Regarding the manner of electing the President, at the opening of the Convention Mason said that he should like to see him popularly elected, but that such a procedure was impracticable; later he thought it also undesirable. In July, he made a comprehensive speech reviewing the various plans that had been proposed, with the conclusion that election by the legislature was perhaps the best suggestion.

Mason made fewer speeches on the judiciary than on the other two branches. He disapproved the nomination of judges by the executive with the concurrence of two-thirds of the Senate as being in practice nomination by the President. In proposing to associate the judges with the President as a revisionary council, he favored endowing them with the power to determine the constitutionality of a law in general as well as in a specific case.

Among his many proposals concerning the powers of the legislature, Mason strongly advocated placement of power over money bills in the popularly elected House, and prohibition of provisions for perpetual revenue. Though he well understood the evils of inflation, he resisted tying the government's hands in the matter of emitting bills of credit as likely to prove embarrassing in grave emergencies; at the same time he attempted to safeguard against speculative operations in the present currency. At several points he announced himself in favor of sumptuary laws. He was against standing armies, but clearly aware of the necessity of unifying the national defense; he strongly approved central regulation of the militia. He proposed that the seat of government, as soon as suitable buildings could be erected, should be located elsewhere than at a state capital.

Each time that the question of the terms on which new states should be admitted came up, he stood firm for equality of privileges for the inhabitants of the Northwest Territory, combatting the exclusiveness of those who wished to perpetuate seaboard dominance over the inchoate but indubitable power of the land beyond the hills.

Mason disapproved of giving to Congress the power to initiate amendments; he was convinced that if placed there, it would never be exercised. He insisted that the Constitution should be ratified by the people of the states in convention rather than by their legislatures; the new frame of government should be put into operation as soon as nine states had ratified it.

After the navigation act-slave trade bargain, however, Mason began to have reservations about the Constitution. They were shared by his colleague, Governor Edmund Randolph. On September 10, after stating his objections fully, Randolph moved that the Constitution as so far framed should not be considered final; but after being passed on to Congress and the states for their consideration, should be returned with suggestions for review by a second convention.

Mason, who had not yet despaired of altering the provisions he found objectionable, urged Randolph to postpone his motion while he made a final effort to secure changes. The most vigorous of his efforts, in conjunction with Gerry of Massachusetts, was to get a bill of rights inserted. He failed. Consequently, when Randolph repeated his motion on September 15, Mason seconded it by his last speech in the Convention:

This Constitution had been formed without the knowledge or idea of the people. A second convention will know more of the sense of the people, and be able to provide a system more consonant to it. It was improper to say to the people, take this or nothing. As the Constitution now stands, he could neither give it his support or vote in Virginia; and he could not sign here what he could not support there. With the expedient of another convention, as proposed, he could sign.

Two days later, September 17, Franklin rose at the beginning of business to initiate the final ceremony. While admitting the faults of the document before them, he urged its signature on the grounds of its being the best available: "Thus I consent, Sir, to this Constitution because I expect no better, and because I am not sure that it is not the best. . . ."

Concluding, he suggested a formula originating with Gouverneur Morris, by which it was hoped to get every member present to sign. Since the majority of the delegates from each state favored the document, it was to be attested as "Done in Convention by the unanimous consent of *the States* present." The ambiguity proved inacceptable, however; both Randolph and Gerry said that they regarded their signatures as committing them to the document, and while the former held open his decision as to whether he would subsequently support it, both of them, with Mason, withheld their names.

XIII

MASON IN OPPOSITION

As soon as the Philadelphia assemblage adjourned, the lines for and against ratification of the Constitution began to be drawn. Pennsylvania set an early date for a state convention, and most of the other states followed rapidly. Through letters and pamphlets by the score, partisans sought to persuade state majorities of the soundness of their respective sides. In Pennsylvania, the *Independent Gazetteer* brought out the anti-Constitution opinions of "Centinel"; in New York Hamilton, Madison, and Jay urged ratification in the "Federalist."

As soon as he reached home, Washington began a correspondence with strategic leaders in Virginia. The tone of his first letters is mild; writing to Patrick Henry on September 24, 1787, he contented himself with saying:

I wish the constitution which is offered, had been made more perfect; but I sincerely believe it is the best that could be obtained at this time. And, as a constitutional door is opened for amendment hereafter, the adoption of it, under the present circumstances of the Union, is in my opinion desirable.

By January 8, in influencing Randolph he was taking a firmer line:

There are some things in the new form, I will readily acknowledge wch never did, and I am persuaded never will, obtain my cordial approbation; but I then did conceive, and now do most firmly believe, that, in the aggregate, it

[59]

is the best Constitution that can be obtained at this Epocha; and that this, or a dissolution of the Union awaits our choice. Thus believing, I had not, nor have I now any hesitation in deciding on which to lean.

Mason, in turn, sent Washington his "Objections to the Proposed Constitution," but though the two exchanged considerable correspondence while Mason was away in the Assembly, Washington made no reference to it nor any effort to change the attitude of his neighbor. Richard Henry Lee's "Observations leading to a Fair Examination of the System of Government proposed by the late Convention," a letter from Randolph stating the position from which he later departed, and Mason's "Objections" made up the chief anti-Constitution literature in Virginia.

The "Objections" were outlined while Mason was still in Philadelphia; they recapitulated the motions which he regarded as essential but which had been lost in debate, calling particular attention to the absence of a bill of rights, the small size of the House of Representatives, the power of the Senate over money bills and its close connection with the executive in regard to appointments, the provision for a vice-president, the failure to provide a privy council to advise the executive, the over-extensive jurisdiction of the federal judiciary, and the powers given to Congress in respect to trade and navigation laws, but withheld from it for twenty years in respect to the traffic in slaves.

To Jefferson, in France, Mason wrote:

I make no doubt that you have long ago received Copys of the new Constitution of Government . . . Upon the most mature Consideration I was capable of, and from motives of sincere Patriotism, I was under the necessity of refusing my signature . . . and drew up some general Objections; which I intended to offer, by way of protest; but was discouraged . . . after the Patrons of this new plan found they had a decided majority in their Favour, . . . obtained by a Compromise between the Eastern and the two Southern States, to permit the latter to continue the Importation of Slaves for twenty odd years; a more favorite Object with them than the Liberty and Happiness of the People.

The Virginia ratifying convention was called to meet at Richmond the second day of June; the contest for seats was spirited. Washington's statement that the people in his vicinity were Federalist to a man doubtless explains why Mason sought election from Stafford rather than Fairfax County.

Mason's opposition required physical courage. According to legend, the mayor of Alexandria warned him that the public mind was so inflamed as to render his presence in the town unsafe; Mason immediately demanded that the crier be sent out to call a town assembly, announcing that George Mason would address the people from the courthouse steps. He took his stand there and allowed the citizens to gather; when they had come he succinctly outlined his objections to the Constitution as proposed; so imposing was his calm that when he had finished he parted an awestruck crowd to mount his horse and ride untouched away. And to a Federalist heckler in Stafford, who shouted: "Mr. Mason, you are an old man, and the public notices that you are losing your faculties," he retorted "Sir, the public will never notice when you lose yours."

By the time the Convention gathered in Richmond, the forces in favor of ratification had been greatly strengthened by the national political situation. Eight states had already ratified, and the assent of a ninth, which would bring the new system into effect, was momentarily antici- pated. Since the ratifying states were scattered the entire length of the coast, no chance for rival blocs existed; any state refusing to come in under the so-called "New Roof" would simply be left outside to face the weather. In addition, there was a tacit probability, amount- ing to practical certainty, that if Virginia acceded before the new gov- ernment was organized, the first President would be George Washing- ton; if not, the first President would come from the North.

The state political situation was less clear-cut. In 1776, the conven- tion that framed the constitution of Virginia had opened with the forces of Henry opposing the forces of Pendleton; when the convention that ratified the Federal Constitution gathered in 1789, Pendleton's crutch symbolized his general physical frailty, and Henry's wig twirled on his forefinger with an increased testiness that came out in the debates, but as respective commanders of the battalions of order and the volunteers of liberty they had in no way altered. Only, this time, the tides were set the other way.

A passage at arms between them near the opening of the convention summed up their enduring difference. Henry declared, "You will *sip sorrow,* to use a vulgar phrase, if you want any other security than the laws of Virginia;" to which Pendleton replied: "On the subject of gov- ernment the worthy member and myself differ on the threshold. I think government necessary to protect liberty. He supposes the American spirit all-sufficient for the purpose."

When it came to the massing of talent, each side presented a formi- dable array. Among those in favor, Pendleton headed the older gener- ation of lawyers; second only to him in importance was George Wythe, who after long hesitation had recently decided to approve ratification— when the Convention elected officers, Pendleton became president, and Wythe chairman of the Committee of the Whole. Light-Horse Harry Lee led the young military group that had come of age during the war and attributed all its difficulties to the "imbecility of the Confedera- tion." Madison served as constitutionalist, his previous standing en- hanced by the large share he had just taken in the work in Philadelphia; among the younger men were George Nicholas and John Marshall.

These were present in the flesh; a towering influence behind them was Washington. The entire country knew he ardently favored ratification; throughout the proceedings, that knowledge was one of the great intangibles. It was likewise Washington's influence more than any other factor which made it possible for the pro-Constitutionists, at the crucial moment, to bring the Governor of Virginia into their camp. When Edmund Randolph withheld his signature from the Constitution in Philadelphia, he expressly reserved freedom of subsequent action, but his objections there had been so strong that his change of front caused consternation in the ranks of the opposition and gave the affirmative side the exhilaration of an initial victory.

The fact that these various men supported the Constitution for widely different reasons was an asset; their views were cumulative in effect. Quite the contrary was the result of a similar situation in the opposition. Man for man, the two sides very nearly balanced; in Henry the negative had a popular leader; in Mason, a constitutionalist and the principal author of the frame of government under which the people of Virginia were living; in Benjamin Harrison and William Grayson, legislators of reputation; in Tyler and Monroe, promising members of the oncoming generation. But the opposition could not be effective without being united; after Randolph changed sides the most prominent opponents were Henry and Mason, and the bases of their disapproval were fundamentally different. The two friends might walk arm in arm each morning from their rooms at "The Swan" to the Academy on Shockoe Hill, but once inside, their lines diverged. Henry desired to prevent the movement towards continental unity from going beyond the league provided by the Confederation; Mason declared "that although he is for amendments, he will not quit the Union even if they should not be made."

In accordance with this belief, at the very opening of the convention Mason proposed a procedure which delighted Madison and cut the ground from under Henry's feet.

Henry's persuasiveness depended rather directly on addressing a general subject; his dramatic technique was at its height when his cause was capable of simplification into two ringing alternatives, one to be damned and one to be extolled until the emotions of his audience were swung into his mood. Consequently, when Mason rose as soon as the papers from Congress had been read, and moved that the Constitution be taken up clause by clause, Henry was at a disadvantage; and Madison, realizing that under such a procedure negative votes would offer only piecemeal threats to adoption of the document, whereas it could be finished with a single stroke in the case of its consideration as a whole, seconded Mason's motion with alacrity.

Even before the opening of debate, three subjects were assured of a thorough canvass. The detail in which the functions of the judiciary were outlined in the Virginia constitution had shown, twelve years before, which department was considered the crucial feature of a free government; a meticulous scrutiny of the powers of the Federal Supreme Court was therefore to be expected. The other two subjects were closely connected with past politics. The unsound financial transactions of the Confederation were still so fresh in evil memory that the vesting of a power of direct taxation in the central government was certain to be challenged, however much the absence of such a power had been the cause of past abuses. Anxiety as to the future of the western lands raised similar doubts about the treaty power even among those who desired ratification.

Day by day, much of the ground covered in Philadelphia was retraversed. Occasionally, however, there were new interpretations of subsequent importance, like the exchange between Mason and Marshall on one section of the judiciary article. Mason, speaking on the various jurisdictions of the Supreme Court, said of the clause relative "to controversies between a State and citizens of another State":

How will their jurisdiction in this case do? Let the gentleman look to the Westward. Claims respecting those lands, every liquidated account, or other claim against this State, will be tried before the Federal court. Is not this disgraceful? Is the State of Virginia to be brought to the bar of justice like a delinquent individual? Is the sovereignty of the State to be arraigned like a culprit, or a private offender? Will the States undergo this mortification? I think this power perfectly unnecessary.

Madison, in reply, remarked that it would be not in the power of individuals to call a state into court; a few speeches later (after a blanket lamentation by Henry to the effect that now the purse was gone, the sword was gone, and the judges gone) the future chief justice rose and delivered his opinion. Marshall said:

With respect to disputes between a State and citizens of another State, its jurisdiction has been decried with unusual vehemence. I hope no gentleman will think that a State will be called at the bar of the Federal Court . . . It is not rational to suppose that the sovereign power shall be dragged before a court. The intent is to enable States to recover claims of individuals residing in other States. I contend this construction is warranted by the words. I see a difficulty in making a State defendant, which does not prevent its being plaintiff.

But within five years a suit brought against Georgia and another threatened against Massachusetts bore out the correctness of Mason's construction and necessitated the passage, in 1798, of the Eleventh Amendment to the Constitution.

When the treaty-making power of the Senate was considered, another aspect of the western land question—freedom of navigation of the

Mississippi—caused concern among representatives of frontier communities and came close to reversing the final vote.

Almost as heated were the discussions of the tax power. Madison pointed out the danger of trouble with Great Britain; a navy is necessary, and a reliable source of war credits must be found for its support. If the federal government is to be insured of independent supplies, direct tax powers must be vested in it. The advocates of states' rights resisted this proposal, doubting that direct taxes could be equitably applied over so diversified an area as the thirteen states. A determined demand was heard that each commonwealth be allowed to raise its own quota; behind it was the possibility that Congress might overassess the class of property owned exclusively in the South, the slaves. Mason's opposition combined defense of the property rights of the owner in a slave economy with denunciation of slavery as a cancerous institution. As a further safeguard of sectional interest he also urged requirement of a two-thirds majority in voting regulations of commerce and navigation.

During the third week of the debate, the tide began to turn, almost insensibly, towards ratification.

When it became obvious that a decision must soon be made, the convention reports show an alarmist note creeping into the speeches of the opposition. Mason said that "the adoption of a system so replete with defects could not but be productive of the most alarming consequences. He dreaded popular resistance to its operation; . . . he trusted gentlemen would pause before they would decide a question which involved such awful consequences." Grayson, paying a tribute to Washington, expressed doubts concerning the frame of government which he would be called on to inaugurate: "I think that, were it not for one great character in America so many men would not be for this government." Madison urged adoption, if necessary, with amendments to be subsequently incorporated into the body of the law.

Henry then rose for a last major effort. By a romantic fitness, even the elements joined his melodramatic appeal. His peroration began: "Our own happiness alone is not affected by this event. . . . We have it in our power to secure the happiness of half the human race. Its adoption may involve the misery of the other hemispheres. . . ." The rest was destroyed by the sudden crashing of a tremendous thunderstorm, that blanked the windowpanes with driving rain.

Then, as suddenly as it had come, the storm vanished, and, in the clear calm that followed, Nicholas rose and proposed the question for the morning of the next day.

The course of that day's debates was charted by the Federalists with the utmost care. It was clearly recognized that a dozen votes would be decisive. Nicholas was the first speaker; following a form prepared by Wythe, he urged the passage of the Constitution accompanied by a set of subsequent amendments. Tyler, for the opposition, countered by requiring the clerk to read a bill of rights and prior amendments drawn up by Henry. Harrison warned against accepting subsequent amendments; Madison, in a conciliatory reply, declared that all of the friends of the Constitution would help put them through; Monroe maintained that prior amendments alone would be valuable. The Federalists then culminated their appeal in a speech by the young James Innes, selected to counterbalance Henry, since his oratory was of the same popularly moving type. The attitude of the Western delegates had been in doubt; two of them now rose and declared they would vote in favor of the Constitution.

The significance of their decision was not lost upon Henry; he accepted the olive branch which Nicholas and Madison had offered: "I will not go on to violence but will wait with hopes that the spirit which predominated in the Revolution is not yet lost." Randolph ended the debate; the Committee of the Whole became the Convention. A resolution was offered in favor of ratification, with amendments proposed for consideration immediately the new government was set up.

A substitute resolution, which provided that a declaration of rights and amendments should be submitted to the other states prior to ratification, lost by eight votes. The substantive motion then carried by a majority of 10 in a house of 168. Virginia had joined the United States. Two days later, the Committee on Amendments, of which Mason had been an active member, reported a bill of rights that followed closely Mason's Declaration of 1776, and twenty additional amendments for addition to the document. Pendleton's valedictory speech ended a quarter century of constitution-making in Virginia.

XIV

FINAL RETIREMENT

From his vantage point at Gunston Hall, Mason followed intently the progress of the proposed amendments to the Constitution. The net result of the various ratifying conventions was not very different from what Jefferson had hoped for from France: "I sincerely wish that the 9 first conventions may receive & the last 4 reject it. The former will receive it finally, while the latter will oblige them to offer a declaration of rights in order to complete the union. We shall thus have all its good, and cure its principal defect."

To Mason and Jefferson, the tenth amendment was the most important: "All powers not delegated to the United States by the Constitution, nor prohibited by it to the States, are reserved to the States respectively or to the people." This explicit reservation of powers had been first on the list of amendments proposed by Virginia; it certified the federal character of the national government in defiance of the Hamiltonian forces which were already mustering for consolidation.

The addition of the first amendments did much to soften Mason's attitude towards the Constitution; his relief at their passage is apparent in a letter to Samuel Griffin: "I have received much Satisfaction from the Amendments to the federal Constitution which have lately passed the House of Representatives; I hope they will also pass the Senate. With two or three further Amendments . . . I could cheerfully put my Hand and Heart to the New Government."

In 1790 a final effort was made to bring Mason into office: Richard Henry Lee and William Grayson had been appointed Virginia's first senators; when the latter died, Governor Randolph named Mason in his place; but Mason declined. This time, his retirement was final.

The increasing ill health which he cited as the cause of his inability to serve confined him for weeks on end to the house and even to his room; between attacks he devoted himself again to the interests which centered in Gunston Hall, his crops and his garden, his children and his grandchildren, the course of neighborhood affairs. The tranquility of this final period is reflected in letters such as one he sent to John in France, May 14, 1789:

We have had a mocking bird for you ever since last summer, which is quite tame and domestic, and intended to send it out this spring, but it proves a female, and they seldom sing; this hardly attempts a single note, and therefore we shall not send it abroad, to disgrace its native country. I would turn it out of the cage, but am afraid its liberty, after such long confinement, would only make the poor thing a prey to the first hawk that came in its way. We will endeavor to raise some young ones this summer.

Of Mason's grown children, his eldest, George, was closest to Gunston Hall. This son had inherited the same "violent rheumatic disorder" from which his father was a chronic sufferer. After he had tried various hot springs in Virginia, it was decided in 1779 that he should go to Southern France. Supplied with letters to Franklin and Lafayette, he departed for a four-year sojourn. When he came home and married, his father made him a gift of the Lexington plantation.

George was not the only son to spend some time in France. As soon as the colonies escaped from the British Navigation Acts, it became profitable for Virginians to establish importing houses on the Continent; from 1788 to 1791 John Mason, the fourth son, was a member of the firm of Fenwick & Mason of Bordeaux. His father's letters to him during this absence are the most intimate of Mason's writings that have been preserved; they contain a variety of news and comment, personal and public. As to the family, George and William have just left to enjoy the season at Augusta Springs. Thomson and his family are moving in at Hollin Hall, Thomas is in the Academy at Fredericksburg. Mrs. Mason sends her thanks for the "political fan" and gloves which John sent her. He will please select "a piece of silk, a pattern for your sister Betsy. I would have it a handsome but not a very expensive silk, and depend upon your taste in the choice of it. If trimmings are necessary they should be sent with it, and sewing silk to make it up."

Among public events, Mason recounts the course of the remaining ratifying conventions, the creation of congressional districts in Virginia, Monroe's campaign against Madison in Spotsylvania and Orange. Later, he gives the boundaries which the President has laid out for the Federal City; they include some two thousand acres of his land just above Little Falls. The inception of the French Revolution called forth his sympathy; the chaos of its continuation filled him with misgiving.

John returned to Virginia in 1791, having avoided "the danger of falling into the hands of the Algerines"; he found his father preparing to give him too a plantation, Analostan Island in the Potomac, just off the Virginia shore opposite Georgetown. Christmas of 1791, Mason's last Christmas, saw a reunited family at Gunston Hall.

Some of Mason's other letters at this time reflect a sense of isolation from old friends: "I have no reason to expect my interest will have much weight in the new government, having, as you know, warmly opposed it."

When asked to sponsor an appointment to a consulship, he wrote:

You know the friendship which has long existed (indeed from our early youth) between General Washington and myself. I believe there are few men in whom he placed greater confidence; but it is possible my opposition to the new government, both as a member of the national and of the Virginia Convention, may have altered the case.

Madison's feelings towards him caused him similar concern, though Jefferson firmly dismissed the notion of any coolness:

I had no occasion to sound Mr. Madison on your fears expressed in your letter. I knew before, as possessing his sentiments fully on that subject, that his value for you was undiminished. I have always heard him say that though you and he appeared to differ in your systems, yet you were in truth nearer together than most persons who were classed under the same appellation. You may quiet yourself in the assurance of possessing his complete esteem.

Jefferson's judgment as to the personal respect of these men for Mason was sound. What Mason was experiencing, though time was as yet too short for the real nature of the movement to be indentifiable, was the formation of political parties in America. During the colonial period, the incomplete responsibility of the Burgesses had reduced politics to a struggle of personal faction. In 1776 and the years that followed, the cleavage between Tories and Revolutionaries extended all the way to the recognition of separate sovereignties. The first major difference to exist in America within the same polity was over the federalist-anti-federalist issue. After the establishment of the Constitution, the coalition of all the talents characteristic of the revolutionary quarter century had inevitably to cease. The forces which in the next decades came to be associated with the name of Hamilton drew Washington and Madison in one direction; those which came to be associated with the name of Jefferson exerted their strength in another.

Of the group that gave Jeffersonianism its early significance, Mason was the senior member. For twenty unbroken years, from the first emergence of the Movement Part, at the opening of the Revolution to the time when the Federal Union was an accomplished fact, the two men had been either active collaborators or frequent correspondents. Washington recognized their relationship when he sent to Hamilton Jefferson's critique of his first administration and included also the criticisms of those "among whom may be classed my neighbour and quondam friend, Col. Mason."

On Sunday, September 30, 1792, the two friends canvassed the affairs of the nation for the last time; Jefferson scribbled a cramped paper-full of abbreviations of the subjects over which they ranged. Mason first recalled a series of incidents from the Constitutional Convention; then, turning to contemporary issues, he outlined what he regarded as a desirable alternative to Hamilton's handling of federal finance.

Jefferson's disconnected sentences stop abruptly. Perhaps he perceived that his host was tiring; perhaps it was merely time for him to be on his way, for he was expected at Mount Vernon before starting north. Whether or not he had a premonition of it, when he turned his horse westward through the long September light between the black-cherry rows of the entrance avenue, it was for the last time. A generation of advice, joint action, and agreement was over. A week after this final conversation, the statesman of Gunston Hall was dead.